Using digital resources to enhance language learning – case studies in Italian

Edited by Rosalba Biasini and Anna Proudfoot

Published by Research-publishing.net, a not-for-profit association
Voillans, France, info@research-publishing.net

© 2018 by Editors (collective work)
© 2018 by Authors (individual work)

Using digital resources to enhance language learning – case studies in Italian
Edited by Rosalba Biasini and Anna Proudfoot

Rights: This volume is published under the Attribution-NonCommercial-NoDerivatives International (CC BY-NC-ND) licence; **individual articles may have a different licence**. Under the CC BY-NC-ND licence, the volume is freely available online (https://doi.org/10.14705/rpnet.2018.24.9782490057139) for anybody to read, download, copy, and redistribute provided that the author(s), editorial team, and publisher are properly cited. Commercial use and derivative works are, however, not permitted.

Disclaimer: Research-publishing.net does not take any responsibility for the content of the pages written by the authors of this book. The authors have recognised that the work described was not published before, or that it was not under consideration for publication elsewhere. While the information in this book is believed to be true and accurate on the date of its going to press, neither the editorial team nor the publisher can accept any legal responsibility for any errors or omissions. The publisher makes no warranty, expressed or implied, with respect to the material contained herein. While Research-publishing.net is committed to publishing works of integrity, the words are the authors' alone.

Trademark notice: product or corporate names may be trademarks or registered trademarks, and are used only for identification and explanation without intent to infringe.

Copyrighted material: every effort has been made by the editorial team to trace copyright holders and to obtain their permission for the use of copyrighted material in this book. In the event of errors or omissions, please notify the publisher of any corrections that will need to be incorporated in future editions of this book.

Typeset by Research-publishing.net
Cover design by © Raphaël Savina (raphael@savina.net)

ISBN13: 978-2-490057-13-9 (Ebook, PDF, colour)
ISBN13: 978-2-490057-14-6 (Ebook, EPUB, colour)
ISBN13: 978-2-490057-12-2 (Paperback - Print on demand, black and white)
Print on demand technology is a high-quality, innovative and ecological printing method; with which the book is never 'out of stock' or 'out of print'.

British Library Cataloguing-in-Publication Data.
A cataloguing record for this book is available from the British Library.

Legal deposit, UK: British Library.
Legal deposit, France: Bibliothèque Nationale de France - Dépôt légal: juillet 2018.

Table of contents

iv Notes on contributors

1   Introduction to using digital resources to enhance language learning – case studies in Italian
    Rosalba Biasini and Anna Proudfoot

5   Developing pragmatic competence through language digital resources
    Marta Kaliska

17 Enhancing written language skills during the year abroad through online independent learning
    Maria Chiara La Sala

29 Using online tools and resources to encourage independent learning amongst ab initio students of Italian: a case study
    Paola Celant

43 ITALO (MyLearning Log): a case study in the use of technology-based resources to foster student engagement and autonomy
    Salvatore Campisi

55 The Italian electronic language log: a critical evaluation
    Simone Lomartire

67 Using, adapting, and sharing learning resources to widen participation in language learning: a case study of Italian open educational resources for dyslexic students
    Anna Motzo

81 Peer-teaching with technology: an Italian grammar case study
    Marcella Oliviero and Andrea Zhok

95 The digital world as a topic: developing digital competences in the Italian language class
    Rosalba Biasini

107 Author index

Notes on contributors

Editors

Rosalba Biasini graduated in Lettere Classiche (L'Aquila, Italy, 2004). She holds an MA in Translation Studies (Manchester 2005), a D.Phil. in Italian (Oxford 2010) and a Master in Didactics of Italian as a Foreign Language (Ca' Foscari, Venezia 2013). Rosalba is Lecturer in Italian at the University of Liverpool where she teaches Italian language and culture. Her research interests span from literature of the Italian Resistance to didactics of Italian as a foreign language, with a special focus on the use of translation.

Anna Proudfoot is Head of Italian in the School of Languages and Applied Linguistics at the Open University. She developed print and online materials for the Beginners' Italian and Intermediate Italian modules and also contributes to the MA in Translation. She is currently Lead Educator on the OU-Future Learn Italian for Beginners' MOOCs, and recently collaborated with the BBC on the programme Rome Unpacked. Anna has published several Italian grammar and language learning texts. Her research focusses on student engagement in online language learning.

Authors

Salvatore Campisi is Senior Language Tutor at the University of Manchester, where he teaches Italian and coordinates six other languages. He is also an External Examiner at the University of Reading and has formerly taught Italian at the University of Leeds and the University of Salford, where he was awarded a Ph.D. in German literature in 2011. He has a keen interest in the development of web-based and e-learning resources, and his previous publications include both academic and creative work.

Paola Celant graduated in Modern Languages at the University of Udine (Italy) with the equivalent of an MA (1997). She obtained her Italian Qualified Teacher Status (PGCE equivalent) in the year 2000. She has taught Italian language at various levels and institutions in England and Wales: primary, secondary, further, and higher education. Paola Celant is currently working at the Department of Italian in the School of Modern Languages at Bristol University as Language Teaching Fellow.

Marta Kaliska is an assistant professor at the Faculty of Applied Linguistics at the University of Warsaw. In the years 2004-2011, she worked at the Department of Italian Studies, where she obtained a Ph.D. degree in linguistics. Her dissertation concerned the lexical features of young people's language in Italy and in Poland. Currently, her research interests focus on Italian language teaching, the action-oriented approach, specialised translation, and intercultural competence development. She is the co-author of the series of Italian course books for Polish Junior High Schools "Va bene!".

Maria Chiara La Sala graduated in 1991 from the University of Rome 'La Sapienza' in Modern Languages and Literatures. In 2004 she completed a Ph.D. on Italian Sociolinguistics at the University of Leeds. Maria Chiara has taken on the roles of Language Coordinator and School Residence Abroad Coordinator. Currently, she is conducting an investigation on the standards to be attained at successive stages of learning and has incorporated the Common European Framework of Reference for Languages into her language teaching.

Simone Lomartire teaches at all levels of the undergraduate curriculum in Italian and within the Languages for All programme at the Universities of Leeds. He holds an MA degree in Irish Studies (Catholic University of Milan), an MA in Colonial and Postcolonial Studies (Leeds), and a PGCHE from Leeds Beckett University. In 2014, he completed his Ph.D. in English. Simone has published in the area of memoir writing in Ireland, Canadian theatre, and Italian language teaching. The scholarship of teaching now occupies most of his research interests.

Anna Motzo is Lecturer in Italian at the School of Languages and Applied Linguistics at the Open University. Her research interests focus on innovative pedagogies in online language learning. As a doctoral researcher, Anna is currently studying the phenomenon of using language learning social networks

Notes on contributors

in order to learn or practise languages informally. She has (co)authored a number of online language learning resources, including FutureLearn's Italian for Beginners suite of six MOOCs.

Marcella Oliviero is Language Teaching Fellow in Italian at Bristol where she teaches across the whole programme. She is actively involved in innovative practices and has made significant contributions to developing the teaching of Italian at UG and institution-wide levels. Her research interests include peer-teaching, blended-learning, development of students' transferable skills, and open education. She has gained international recognition for her work on peer-teaching and technology enhanced learning of grammar with the APEREO Teaching and Learning Award 2016.

Andrea Zhok (PGCE, Wales; Dip Trans IoL) is Language Director in Italian at the School of Modern Languages, University of Bristol, UK, where he oversees all aspects of the Italian language programme – both at degree and institution-wide levels. He has pursued a broad range of interests in the field of language pedagogy, including projects on assessment, blended learning, translation, employability, and teacher training. The peer-teaching Italian grammar project presented in this publication won the APEREO Teaching and Learning Award (ATLAS) 2016. With almost twenty years' experience, he has gained recognition as a leading figure in the sector. He also works as a translator and interpreter.

Reviewers

Catherine Chabert, Ph.D., has spent most of her academic career designing and implementing language courses and programmes for university students. An early adopter of the CEFR in the UK, she now chairs the steering group of the new UNILANG recognition scheme. She is the director of Languages for All at Cardiff University which is a university-wide programme designed to be flexible (modes of delivery, use of digital technology) and to enhance students' language skills, intercultural understanding, and employment prospects.

Notes on contributors

Chiara Cirillo, Ph.D., is Associate Professor in Second Language Education and Director of the IWLP at the University of Reading. Her research background is in sociolinguistics, with a focus on gender and language. Over her twenty-year career in HE, she has taught Italian language and culture and developed an expertise in pedagogies in tertiary education. Her main areas are assessment, intercultural competence, and teacher development. Dr Cirillo is Senior Fellow of the HEA and an executive committee member of the Association of University Language Centres (AULC).

Silvia Colaiacomo, Ph.D., currently Curriculum and Academic Developer at the University of Kent, worked for nine years at the Modern Language Centre of King's College London as a lecturer and deputy-team leader of Italian and Linguistics. Silvia has also been External Examiner of Italian for different universities in the UK, as well as a subject expert for OFQUAL. Silvia's interests are in international education and intercultural competence and how these are reflected in different approaches to and forms of assessment.

Sonia Cunico is Director of Language Teaching for the Department of Modern Languages and the Foreign Language Centre and Associate Professor at the University of Exeter where she has worked since September 2010. She has extensive experience in innovative curricula development in language learning, developing autonomous learning through Peer Assisted Learning and Language Tandem, as well as in teaching Italian as L2 to UK undergraduates, Translation Studies at MA level, and as a teacher trainer. Sonia's research interests are MFL in Higher Education, Teacher Education, and Intercultural Competence.

Caterina Guardamagna is Lecturer in English Language and Linguistics at the University of Liverpool. Her doctoral research focussed on the Latin expression "secundum NP" ("according to NP") from a cognitive-constructional viewpoint. More recently, she has been exploring politeness in Latin with a corpus-based discourse analytical perspective. Her studies to date include Latin, Italian, and English.

Benoît Guilbaud works as Teaching Fellow at the Sussex Centre for Language Studies (SCLS), where he teaches French language and translation on degree

Notes on contributors

courses in Languages and Language elective modules. He has previously worked at the University of Manchester and Manchester Metropolitan University. He holds an MA and BA from the Université Blaise-Pascal in Clermont-Ferrand (France), a PGCE from Cardiff University, and a PGCAP from Manchester Metropolitan University. He has previously taught on modules in French for medicine, business, and law, as well as general French language, translation, and interpreting. He has presented at a number of conferences on the topics of language teaching, digital literacy, and networked learning. He occasionally tweets as @BenGuilbaud.

Jordi Sanchez-Carrion is Lecturer in Spanish at the University of Liverpool, teaching a range of levels from undergraduate students to advanced students in their first year. Jordi has an extensive experience teaching Spanish and Catalan as a foreign language at the Instituto Cervantes in Manchester and Manchester Metropolitan University, and has taught proficiency courses on different topics related to Spain and Latin America. Jordi is also very interested in the use of technology as a means of blended learning and right now is researching in this field as well as the use of flipped classrooms in HE.

Enza Siciliano Verruccio coordinates language teaching at the Department of Modern Languages and European Studies at the University of Reading, where she has been working for the past 16 years. As holder of the Language Teaching portfolio for the Society for Italian Studies (2010-15), she was responsible for promoting and supporting the development of an active community of Italian language teaching practitioners and researchers in the UK. She specialises in the role of explicit instruction and SLA, ab initio language teaching and learning, and TELL.

Ursula Stickler is Senior Lecturer in German in the School of Languages and Applied Linguistics at the Open University, UK. Her research focusses on independent and technology enhanced language learning and teacher training. She has also published widely in the areas of Tandem learning, qualitative methods for Computer Assisted Language Learning (CALL) research, and eyetracking. She is co-editor of the System Journal.

Sascha Stollhans holds degrees in Germanic and Romance Linguistics, and Second Language Acquisition/Language Teaching. He has taught German in Germany, France, South Africa, and the UK. From 2013-2016, he was a DAAD-Lektor at the University of Nottingham, where he received the prestigious Lord Dearing Award for teaching excellence. Until January 2018, he was Teaching Assistant in Linguistics and German Language Tutor at the University of Manchester. He now works in the translation industry.

1. Introduction to using digital resources to enhance language learning – case studies in Italian

Rosalba Biasini[1] and Anna Proudfoot[2]

In 2015, Anna Proudfoot, Enza Siciliano, and Rosalba Biasini agreed with the Society for Italian Studies (SIS) that a double session dedicated to Italian language teaching and learning would be included in the programme of every SIS Biennial Conference. SIS's stated aim, after all, is "to further the study of Italy, Italian language, literature, film, thought, history, society and arts in the United Kingdom and Ireland" (SIS NA)[3], and guaranteeing a dedicated session at this conference meant creating a space where language tutors and practitioners could present their scholarship and share experiences, methods, and techniques.

The double session at the 2015 conference, held in Oxford, focussed on digital resources and online learning, and was divided into a panel on *Online learning in the Italian language curriculum*, chaired by Anna Proudfoot, and another panel on *Using digital resources to enhance Italian language learning*, chaired by Rosalba Biasini. The topic, central in current research in the field of language teaching and learning, was chosen in order to showcase the specific contribution made by Italian to digital scholarship and innovation.

A group of Italian language tutors attended the conference to present papers and/or to contribute to the discussion on Italian language teaching and learning, and on related scholarship. Following the conference, the group decided that a publication of the proceedings to mark the first of these meetings would be a

---

1. University of Liverpool, Liverpool, United Kingdom; rosalba.biasini@liverpool.ac.uk

2. The Open University, Milton Keynes, United Kingdom; anna.proudfoot@open.ac.uk

3. For more information: https://italianstudies.org.uk/the-society/.

How to cite this chapter: Biasini, R., & Proudfoot, A. (2018). Introduction to using digital resources to enhance language learning – case studies in Italian. In R. Biasini & A. Proudfoot (Eds), *Using digital resources to enhance language learning – case studies in Italian* (pp. 1-3). Research-publishing.net. https://doi.org/10.14705/rpnet.2018.24.793

useful resource for all language tutors. To five of the original papers presented in Oxford, another three were added in order to include a range of ideas and experiences in one publication. The group worked together to produce the book that we are now pleased to present.

The first paper, **Marta Kaliska**'s *Developing pragmatic competence through language digital resources*, provides examples of tasks created on the basis of digital language resources such as language corpora, online forums, and communities, where learners can observe language used in digital communication in order both to attain pragmatic knowledge and enhance their language skills.

The second paper, **Maria Chiara La Sala**'s *Enhancing written language skills during the year abroad through online independent learning*, focusses on online independent language learning resources for the year abroad in Italy, which increases linguistic proficiency and cultural awareness, and seeks to explore how Virtual Learning Environments (VLEs) can allow tutors to support the development of written language skills in the Study Abroad context, evaluating an online resource designed to enhance written language skills during the year abroad.

The next paper, **Paola Celant**'s *Using online tools and resources to encourage independent learning amongst ab initio students of Italian: a case study*, analyses the use of a range of online tools and resources, describing how technology has been embedded in an Italian language course and evaluating to what extent implementation of online tools and resources can enhance the students' experience.

The following two papers explore the use of technology-based language logs to enhance independent learning. **Salvatore Campisi**'s *ITALO (MyLearning Log): a case study in the use of technology-based resources to foster student engagement and autonomy* describes the project 'ITALO (MyLearning Log)', a learning log aimed at encouraging student engagement with the VLE, monitoring usage and effectiveness of the resources deployed, and developing learner autonomy.

Simone Lomartire's *The Italian electronic language log: a critical evaluation* focusses on the use of the electronic language log as a tool to monitor independent learning practices by *ab initio* students, providing a direct analysis and critical evaluation of the work produced by students for their electronic language log and, specifically, showing how this learning tool has helped beginner students of Italian manage their own learning independently.

Anna Motzo's *Using, adapting, and sharing learning resources to widen participation in language learning: a case study of Italian open educational resources for dyslexic students* offers an insight from the perspective of the practitioner on how to use, re-use, and adapt existing language learning materials, namely open educational resources, in ways that are designed to improve the learning experience for dyslexic learners and benefit non-dyslexic learners at the same time by adopting a multisensory structured language approach.

Marcella Oliviero and **Andrea Zhok**'s paper *Peer-teaching with technology: an Italian grammar case study* centres on the notion that changing traditional student identities by turning them into 'student-teachers' can have very positive consequences on their involvement with the learning process. In this approach, students are asked to research a grammar topic and generate tutorials using open-source suite *Xerte*, working collaboratively in small groups and teaching their peers by delivering their own tutorials in class.

The last paper of the publication is **Rosalba Biasini**'s *The digital world as topic: developing digital competences in the Italian language class*, which analyses how digital technologies and competences can be used in the Italian language class as a topic, describing how, while developing all the 'canonical' linguistic skills, students can improve transferable skills, such as working on self-development, shaping digital identity and reputation, and approaching media literacies and learning.

Buona lettura!

2. Developing pragmatic competence through language digital resources

Marta Kaliska[1]

Abstract

According to Kasper (1992), L2 pragmatic knowledge affects all communicative acts. It can be described as the speaker's ability both to adapt linguistic formulae to social contextual constraints and to understand the implications of indirect utterances. The Common European Framework of Reference for languages (CEFR) describes pragmatic competence as an integral component of communicative language competence. It relates to "the functional use of linguistic resources, production of language functions, speech acts, drawing on scenarios or scripts of interactional exchanges; it also concerns the mastery of discourse, cohesion and coherence, the identification of text types and forms, irony and parody" (CEFR, 2001, p. 13). The present article aims at providing some useful examples of tasks created on the basis of language digital resources, such as language corpora, online forums, and communities where learners can observe language used in digital communication in order both to attain pragmatic knowledge and enhance their language skills. The proposed tasks were implemented in the Italian courses at B1/B2 level organised by the Faculty of Applied Linguistics at the University of Warsaw in the years 2014-2015. Such tasks constituted additional activities within a conversational module focused on developing communicative competence in which pragmatic abilities and sociocultural knowledge play a crucial role.

Keywords: pragmatic competence, Italian language teaching, digital resources, action-oriented approach, classroom learning.

---

1. Warsaw University, Warsaw, Poland; m.kaliska@uw.edu.pl

How to cite this chapter: Kaliska, M. (2018). Developing pragmatic competence through language digital resources. In R. Biasini & A. Proudfoot (Eds), *Using digital resources to enhance language learning – case studies in Italian* (pp. 5-15). Research-publishing.net. https://doi.org/10.14705/rpnet.2018.24.794

1. Introduction

In recent years, European institutions, and in particular the Council of Europe, have endeavoured to introduce multilingual and plurilingual policies at every stage of education. The policies aim at promoting linguistic diversification and life-long learning in order to facilitate communication between different nations, focusing on cultural, vocational, and other personal needs. The Council of Europe language policies are supported by the CEFR, which describes and defines six levels of language ability (CEFR, 2001).

Pragmatic competence constitutes an integral element of communicative competence in a foreign language, which, according to the CEFR, consists of three main components: linguistic, sociolinguistic, and pragmatic competences (CEFR, 2001, p. 108). Its balanced development enriches learners' general knowledge and skills so that they are able to use a foreign language appropriately in a given situation. The question posed in the present article is how to teach and how to maximise pragmatic competence development in Italian as a foreign language through online resources.

2. Theory and methodology

2.1. Pragmatic competence

According to Kasper (1992), pragmatic knowledge affects all communicative acts regardless of the language used. It can be described as the ability of the speaker both to adapt linguistic formulae to social contextual constraints and to understand the implications of indirect utterances. The development of pragmatic competence depends on general communicative knowledge and interactional opportunities to: (1) practise the target language, allowing learners to demonstrate their skills; (2) receive constructive feedback; and (3) observe linguistic input. In comparison with the CEFR's recommendations, Bachman (1990) states that pragmatic competence refers to illocutionary abilities (i.e. speech strategies, language functions, pragmatic routines) and sociolinguistic abilities (i.e. socially acceptable linguistic/cultural behaviour in a given context), and is an integrative component of general language competence.

When foreign language pragmatic information is insufficient, learners develop their own pragmatic interlanguage, transferring knowledge from the first language or from universal knowledge to their linguistic performance in a foreign language, which may cause a pragmatic failure of a communication act (Kasper, 1992). Current research suggests that learners who receive explicit pragmatic instruction outperform those who are only exposed to linguistic input without such information (Bardovi-Harlig, 2001; Olshtain & Cohen, 1990).

2.2. Action-oriented approach to foreign language teaching

The action-oriented approach, recommended by the CEFR, fulfils the current needs of modern language teaching. It "views users and learners of a language primarily as 'social agents', i.e. members of society who have tasks (not exclusively language-related) to accomplish in a given set of circumstances" (CEFR, 2001, p. 9). The action-oriented approach is mainly embodied in task-based teaching, where students learn by doing, and which provides a stimulus for experiencing a foreign language (Piccardo, 2010; Willis, 1996). The task is defined as "any purposeful action considered by an individual as necessary in order to achieve a given result in the context of a problem to be solved, an obligation to fulfil or an objective to be achieved" (CEFR, 2001, p. 10). The nature of the task can vary in creativity, complexity, and level of language difficulty. The notion of *task* is similar to *activity* (Piccardo, 2014).

2.3. Pragmatic competence development in the classroom

As far as language teaching is concerned, there is the problem of how to teach pragmatic competence. Pragmatic instruction should be introduced explicitly in order to help students understand certain language subtleties, then correctly interpret them. It is advisable to use authentic language examples and to introduce a classroom discussion which explores pragmatic differences in order to raise students' awareness (Bardovi-Harlig & Mahan-Taylor 2003,

p. 38). Designing tasks based on digital language resources promises to be a very creative process for tutors as well as learners. The materials are available at any time, and the type of language used in online forums, chat-lines, or social media often consists of features typical of spoken, written, and online language suitable for communicative competence development, including also pragmatic competence. The implementation of such didactic tasks falls within online teaching, a subject area which has been broadly analysed by many scholars such as Warschauer (1997), Furstenberg (1997), and Mezzadri (2001). As stated by Warschauer, Shetzer, and Meloni (2000), online resources represent a very useful language tool for creating differentiated teaching tasks that support collaborative learning and individual research by students, while also requiring innovative pedagogical practices and technological competence (Furstenberg, 1997; Hampel, 2006).

Such tasks targeted at pragmatic competence development prove to be extremely useful because of their innovative character. Tutors can create didactic materials which meet learners' particular communication goals in contrast with traditional textbooks which present fixed content that can neither be updated nor tailored to a rapidly changing sociocultural reality. To a certain extent, pragmatic knowledge can be built by observing authentic text samples and skills can be taught by inviting learners to take part in activities that require their involvement and effective language use.

3. Results: developing tasks

The present article aims at providing certain task examples focused on the development of pragmatic competence through observation and active participation on the basis of given online resources, such as Italian language corpora available on the Internet, forums, and online communities. In the present article, the notion of task refers to the definition proposed by the CEFR (2001): "any purposeful action considered by an individual as necessary in order to achieve a given result in the context of a problem to be solved, an obligation to fulfil or an objective to be achieved" (p. 10), but also to the concept of a pedagogical task explained by Willis and Willis (2001) as a "classroom undertaking where the target language is used by the learner for a communicative purpose in order to achieve an outcome" (p. 173). The CEFR definition is very generic in character, allowing its integration according to students' learning needs, while Willis' pedagogical task emphasises communicative goals – especially required to develop the pragmatic competence.

The following tasks were designed and developed for two groups of 15 students, level B1-B2 in Italian, in their third year of the undergraduate degree at the Faculty of Applied Linguistics, University of Warsaw, in the academic year 2014-2015. They were implemented within the conversation module which has 30 contact hours of scheduled teaching in the classroom per semester. The objective was to provide students with the pragmatic explicit information in Italian, the lack of which may constitute a problematic issue for Polish-speaking students coming from a diverse cultural background.

As far as language corpora are concerned, the text samples selected for pragmatic goals should have an interactive nature, and be representative of spoken language in which learners can observe specific elements. These tasks enhance learners' creativity and autonomy, promoting student-led discovery learning and research (Aston, 2001). The tutor's task is to select the corpus extracts, indicate the required structures or expressions, and give initial instructions, but the main task, which involves observation, identification, and reapplication, is carried out by learners who, working in pairs or in small groups, firstly analyse the given text samples with regard to pragmatic functions and then present the outcomes in the classroom. The last phase consists in the reapplication of the learnt forms which may be accomplished by teaching techniques, such as dramatisation of the discussed dialogues, role-making focused on given pragmatic goals, taking part in online information exchange, and commenting or writing their own requests or questions.

The first task was developed on the basis of Zorzi's (2001) research concerning the pedagogical use of a spoken Italian corpus (LIP: Lessico di Frequenza dell'Italiano Parlato). The task involved the observation and investigation of

Chapter 2

Italian discourse markers used within given situational contexts. These markers play a significant role in Italian language communication, therefore within Italian language classes a particular focus should be put on their meaning and usage.

Task 1. Osservate e analizzate i significati dei seguenti segnali discorsivi / Observe and analyse the meaning of the following discourse markers.

A: ecco # ah ma avevi ragione tu in aula occupata accanto al bar a Sergio o a Ester

B: proviamo

A: cosa *

B: devo trovare Marco prima che % la Corte dei Conti % provo dopo pranzo

A: no no

B: cioè volevo chiamare Marco prima che chiuda la Corte dei Conti però mi sa che ormai so' già andati via vero

A: boh che ore sono *

A: ma dai il primo giorno se ci pensi te lo ricordi il primo giorno

A: ah allora proviamo dai

The students were asked to discuss and make hypotheses about the meaning of the highlighted words, taking into account the situational context of the dialogue. The tutor's objective was to draw their attention to given discourse markers which are typical of Italian language. Then, the students were invited to reflect on possible translations into Polish and whether or not there existed equivalents. The most difficult elements turned out to be markers such as: *boh* and *(ma) dai*, the latter having different meanings according to context, raising further doubts about its correct use. Active observation and a focus on meaning broadens students' knowledge concerning the possible contexts in which a given discourse marker can be used.

The next tasks discussed the realisation of speech acts within a forum community where members exchange tourist information. In general, the language of the forum community offers a great many examples to be analysed in terms of the realisation of selected speech acts. Learners have an opportunity to observe the communication dynamics between the members of such communities, i.e. how they ask questions, explain issues, thank, apologise, joke, give advice, make requests and express different feelings. The second task involves matching given illocutionary functions to the selected posts. Its aims are to show the language structures needed to achieve specific communication goals, and at the same time to invite learners to reflect upon the interaction in Italian.

> **Task 2**. Osservate i seguenti brani. Abbinate una funzione illocutiva a ogni testo / Observe the following texts, then match an illocutionary function to a given post.
>
> CONSIGLIO / RICHIESTA DI INFORMAZIONI / ACCORDO / RIFIUTO
>
> NORA: Ti consiglio di fare la parte lago tutta in giornata e di prendere un biglietto giornaliero: puoi acquistarlo nella prima biglietteria.
>
> GIANNI: Neda, grazie di cuore, ma non posso accettare perché fino ad ora ho rifiutato tutte le nomination ricevute. Ti ringrazio comunque, sei gentile. Un caro saluto.
>
> ALICE: Sono d'accordo. Il mondo va avanti veloce - innovazione, globalizzazione - in alcuni settori giovani di tutto il mondo creano impresa e servizi con mercati mondiali...

Chapter 2

> LUCIA: Vorrei sapere se c´è un limite di tempo entro il quale le segreterie devono rilasciare ai docenti i certificati di servizio richiesti.

After completing the task, the students were asked by the tutor to compare the ways in which such speech acts are realised in both Polish and Italian. The authentic communication context made them more involved in the task that they considered useful and interesting.

Furthermore, in the third task, the learners were asked to observe how community members exchange tourist information, and subsequently, they were invited to write a similar request and post it in the same forum. It allowed learners to participate actively in digital communication acts and gave them an opportunity to interact with other participants, often native Italian speakers.

> **Task 3**. Leggete i seguenti brani. Specificate le strutture linguistiche che servono a richiedere informazioni. In coppia scrivete la vostra richiesta di informazioni riguardo a ristoranti convenienti di Perugia. Inserite la vostra richiesta nel forum: http://www.tripadvisor.it e raccogliete le risposte. / Read the following texts. Then identify the linguistic structures that serve to ask for information. In couples write a short text in which you ask information about affordable restaurants in Perugia. Publish your post in the forum: http://www.tripadvisor.it and collect the answers.

> JOE: Ciao, vorrei qualche informazione sulle escursioni che si possono fare partendo da Lecco. Io e la mia ragazza staremo lì dal 18 al 22 Luglio e oltre a visitare Lecco e diversi paesi (Varenna, Bellagio, etc) ci interesserebbe fare camminate, magari anche in montagna.

> GIOVANNA: Urgente!!! Parto sabato prossimo! vacanza decisa all'ultimo, avevo scelto un'altra destinazione, poi accantonata. Già prenotato hotel a Cernobbio, lette belle recensioni. Domande: non capisco nulla della rete di navigazione dei battelli. Chi mi sa chiarire le idee?

> ALEX: Ciao. Cerco consigli per una giornata a Como. Arriveremmo la mattina da Milano Cadorna a Como Lago Nord.

At the final stage, students also collected posts published as responses to their information request. The task was carried out both in the classroom (observation and writing requests) and as homework (collecting responses or communicating with other forum participants) in order to maximise learning opportunities. Its multidimensional nature aimed at developing students' different abilities, such as: (1) analysing how the speech acts tend to be realised; (2) communicating with native speakers within an online information exchange; and (3) comprehending the received responses. The tutor's main task was to monitor the appropriateness of students' requests.

After completing the tasks, the course participants were invited to discuss their effectiveness. Based on their responses, the subject area and the real-life communication context converged with their interests, which enhanced their involvement in the activity and facilitated the tutor's work. The accomplishment of the third task was rather extended in time, the first analytical part was performed during the lesson, then, the second practical one outside the classroom. The students appreciated both the real life situational context and the opportunity to interact with Italian speakers.

4. Conclusion

This article has attempted to offer some didactic proposals which may provide a pattern for further activities aimed at developing pragmatic competence in relation to such areas of practice as: (1) identifying language forms from a given corpus; (2) identifying and aligning language functions from a given forum exchange; and (3) participating actively in a forum exchange. Their inventiveness depends on tutors' and learners' needs, as well as on the organisational and technical possibilities available in the classroom. After completing the tasks, the tutor discussed the subject area and their effectiveness with the students who gave positive feedback on the digital communication context in which the tasks were collocated. They considered them particularly useful as far as the completion of the given speech acts is concerned.

As stated by Kasper and Rose (2011), a simple exposure to the target language does not imply the development of pragmatic competence. Learners are not able to distinguish certain pragmatic factors related to the communication context only through the observation and analysis of the language input. Digital resources offer Italian tutors an opportunity to create more or less complicated tasks in which they can emphasise structures, collocations, or single words used to express given speech acts or other discursive functions. The action-oriented approach proves an effective method for tutors to design tasks whose main objective is to show pragmatic language features related to real-life communication.

References

Aston, G. (2001). *Learning with corpora: an overview*. Athelstan.
Bachman, L. (1990). *Fundamental considerations in language testing*. Oxford University Press.
Bardovi-Harlig, K. (2001). Empirical evidence of the need for instruction in pragmatics. In K. R. Rose & G. Kasper (Eds), *Pragmatics in language teaching* (pp. 13-32). Cambridge University Press. https://doi.org/10.1017/CBO9781139524797.005
Bardovi-Harlig, K, & Mahan-Taylor. R. (2003). Introduction to teaching pragmatics. *English Teaching Forum, 41*(3), 37-39.
CEFR. (2001). *Common European framework of reference for languages: learning, teaching, assessment*. Council of Europe.
Furstenberg, G. (1997). Teaching with technology: what is at stake? *ADFL Bulletin, 28*(3), 21-25. https://doi.org/10.1632/adfl.28.3.21
Hampel, R. (2006). Rethinking task design for the digital age: a framework for language teaching and learning in a synchronous online environment. *ReCALL, 18*(1), 105-121. https://doi.org/10.1017/S0958344006000711
Kasper, G. (1992). Pragmatic transfer. *Second Language Research, 8*(3), 203-231. https://doi.org/10.1177/026765839200800303

Kasper, G., & Rose, K. R. (2011). The role of instruction in learning second language pragmatics. In L. Ortega (Ed.), *Second language acquisition. Critical concepts in linguistics, Volume VI* (pp. 340-367). Routledge.

Mezzadri, M. (2001). *Internet nella didattica dell'italiano*. Guerra Edizioni.

Olshtain, E., & Cohen, A. D. (1990). The learning of complex speech act behaviour. *TESL Canada Journal, 7*, pp. 45-65. https://doi.org/10.18806/tesl.v7i2.568

Piccardo, E. (2010). From communicative to action-oriented: new perspectives for a new millennium. *TESL Ontario Contact, 36*(2), 20-35.

Piccardo, E. (2014). *From communicative to action-oriented: a research pathway*. CSC Canada.

Warschauer, M. (1997). Computer-mediated collaborative learning: theory and practice. *The Modern Language Journal, 81*(4), 470-481. https://doi.org/10.1111/j.1540-4781.1997.tb05514.x

Warschauer, M., Shetzer, H., & Meloni, C. (2000). Internet for English teaching. *The Electronic Journal for English as a Second Language, 5*(1). http://www.tesl-ej.org/wordpress/issues/volume5/ej17/ej17r17/?wscr

Willis, J. (1996). *A framework for task-based learning*. Longman.

Willis, J., & Willis, D. (2001). Task-based language learning. In R. Carter & D. Nunan (Eds), *The cambridge guide to teaching english to speakers of other languages*. Cambridge University Press. https://doi.org/10.1017/CBO9780511667206.026

Zorzi, D. (2001). The pedagogic use of spoken corpora: learning discourse markers in Italian. In G. Aston (Ed.), *Learning with corpora* (pp. 85-107). Athelstan.

3. Enhancing written language skills during the year abroad through online independent learning

Maria Chiara La Sala[1]

Abstract

This article focusses on the online independent language learning resource for the Year Abroad (YA) in Italy at the University of Leeds. The YA is an important component of most undergraduate degree programmes in Modern Languages. It increases linguistic proficiency and cultural awareness. During the last twenty years, there has been a growing body of research on L2 development of language learners Studying Abroad (SA), which focusses on the acquisition of speaking and listening skills and on intercultural competence, while the development of morpho-syntactic skills remain under researched. This article seeks to explore how Virtual Learning Environments (VLEs) can allow tutors to support the development of written language skills in the SA context. This article evaluates an online resource designed to enhance written language skills during the YA. The outcomes of the initiative will be presented and possible future developments of the online resource will be discussed.

Keywords: independent learning, online resource, written language work, year abroad, study abroad.

---

1. University of Leeds, Leeds, United Kingdom; illmcls@leeds.ac.uk

How to cite this chapter: La Sala, M. C. (2018). Enhancing written language skills during the year abroad through online independent learning. In R. Biasini & A. Proudfoot (Eds), *Using digital resources to enhance language learning – case studies in Italian* (pp. 17-27). Research-publishing.net. https://doi.org/10.14705/rpnet.2018.24.795

1. Introduction

1.1. The context: the YA

The common assumption about SA is that it automatically leads to greater language proficiency. However, current literature does not provide a consistent picture of how the SA experience improves linguistic competence. In particular, there is little evidence that the YA improves morpho-syntactic skills. This could be in part due to the lack of systematic study as students focus on their communicative proficiency whilst abroad.

Technology can provide language tutors with an opportunity to support and guide students' independent learning during their residence abroad. To date, little has been written in this area.

1.2. Background information

As in most British universities where Italian is taught, the undergraduate programme at the University of Leeds has two distinct pathways: Beginners' Programme (BA Italian B) and Advanced Programme (BA Italian A). The cohort of beginners spends one year in Italy as a compulsory part of the degree, whereas the advanced cohort may spend only a term in Italy. The final-year written language exam consists of a translation paper of two literary or journalistic texts: one from English into Italian and one from Italian into English. The second component of the final-year written language exam consists of an essay paper.

For the YA in Italy, students have the following options:

- working as a language assistant with the British Council;

- following an Erasmus study programme at a partner university;

- taking *Corsi Singoli* at a university not included in the Erasmus programme; and

- doing a paid or voluntary work placement.

1.3. The challenge

The need to create a virtual learning environment for YA students derived from two main goals: to facilitate the transition from Level 2 to Level 3 and to give students the opportunity to enhance written language skills during their YA. Despite the common assumption that the period of residence abroad is the best environment to learn a second language (Stern, 1964), students' standards after their period of residence abroad do not always suggest that it has enhanced their written language skills. In Italy, students appear to perfect their speaking, listening, and reading skills, but not their writing. This is due in part to the context of the Italian university where most of the exams are oral and where opportunities for academic writing are rare. Collentine (2009), however, observes that this is a general issue rather than related to specific contexts or institutions:

> "whereas SA (study abroad) affects gains in certain language-specific domains, it does not affect development in all aspects of a learner's competence. Interestingly, linguistic aspects that do indeed seem to benefit from Study Abroad, such as fluency and discursive abilities, are often not those in which AH (at home) FL (foreign language) program directors hope to see improvements, such as those grammatical aspects around which the AH, focus-on-forms syllabus is designed" (p. 224).

2. Methodology

2.1. The YA online resource: Written Language Work (WLW)

The proposed solution to the challenge outlined above was to offer structured guidance for independent learning during the YA through an online resource, the WLW resource.

The first step in the development of the resource was to consider both the objectives and assessment methods of Level 2 and Level 3 language modules as well as the type of environment students were likely to encounter during their YA. The resource was an attempt to link more closely the two contexts for second language acquisition identified by Batstone (2002), the communicative and learning contexts:

> "A communicative context is sociolinguistic in orientation. A learner focuses on the use of language to convey meaning in an appropriate fashion according to contextual cues. The target language is used as a tool to exchange information and participate in important social and interpersonal functions. In contrast, a learning context has a psycholinguistic orientation in which learners focus on form with tutor assistance with the goal of improving their linguistic expertise" (p. 4).

The resource was developed in the academic year 2013-2014 and made available in 2014-2015. Students returning from their YA in September 2015 were the first cohort to use it. It was developed with the assistance of an Erasmus intern, providing a student perspective and a guarantee that the WLW would appeal to a younger generation with digital skills.

The tasks included in the WLW are the following:

- a set of self-correcting grammar exercises;

- a set of self-correcting translation exercises (six of these to be submitted for feedback); and

- a set of writing tasks on an aspect of Italian culture and society with the title 'Compositions' (three of these to be submitted for feedback).

A screenshot of the initial page can be seen below in Figure 1.

Figure 1. Initial page of the WLW

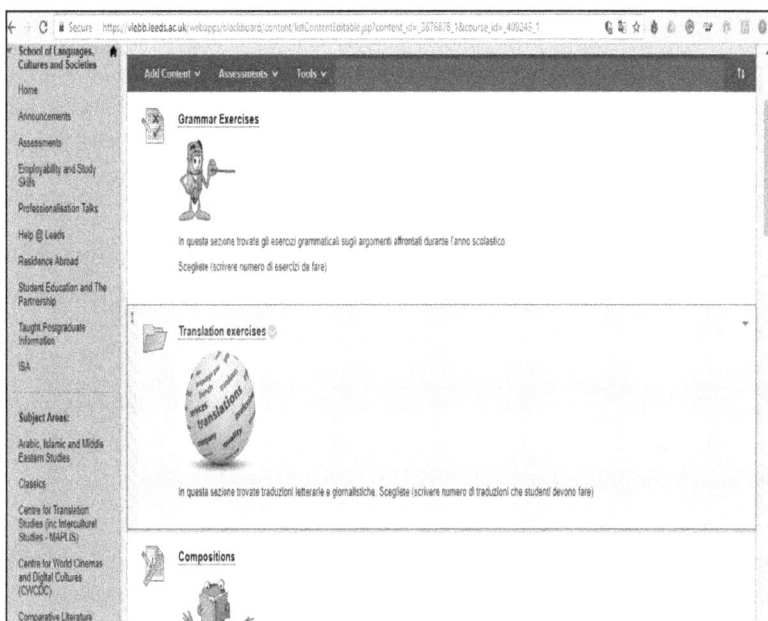

All activities were created within Blackboard Learn, which supports the University of Leeds' VLE, a learning management system familiar to students and therefore involving no additional learning workload. For the self-correcting grammar exercises and translation exercises, the Italian teaching team opted for the Blackboard Test tool, whereas for the compositions, the Blackboard Assignments tool was used. As the latter does not provide appropriate feedback, a more traditional 'one-to-one' feedback is sent to students via individual emails.

In addition to the activities in the WLW, students submit a self-reflective questionnaire and a *resoconto* (a written account) entitled '*La mia permanenza in Italia*' (My stay in Italy), which focusses on the key aspects of the YA experience. These three elements are part of the evaluation for the YA and students, either in a study or work placement, which they must all pass to proceed to their final year.

Chapter 3

2.2. Evaluation of the resource

The WLW was evaluated through student feedback. An online questionnaire[2] with a mix of closed and open questions asked students to what extent the WLW helped them make progress in written language skills and become independent learners. The questionnaire was sent to 39 students and received an 85% response rate (33 students).

The pie chart below (Figure 2) shows that 50% of the respondents thought that using the WLW had enhanced the knowledge and understanding gained from Level 2 written language seminars attended in Year 2.

A possible reason for this relatively low percentage is that the link between the content and assessment methods of the second year language course and those of the final-year language course is not explained clearly enough.

Sixty-two percent of the respondents agreed that assignments and tests available on the WLW are a useful way of making progress in written language skills during the YA (see Figure 3).

Figure 2.   Question 2b

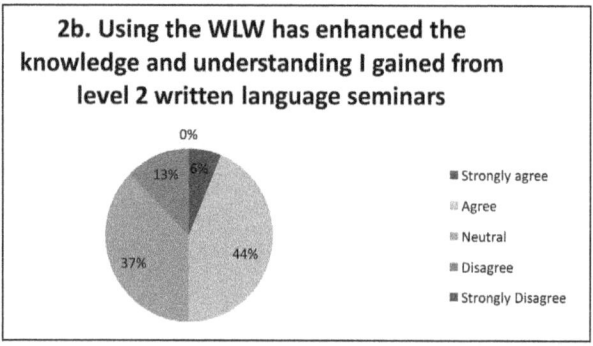

2. https://research-publishing.box.com/s/cihuzkz5v5k71k0511ghrqj1v8snr76e

Figure 3. Question 2c

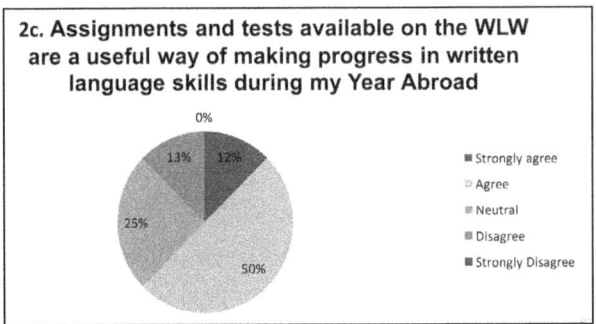

Students' responses to Question 4 are quite varied, see Figure 4.

Figure 4. Question 4

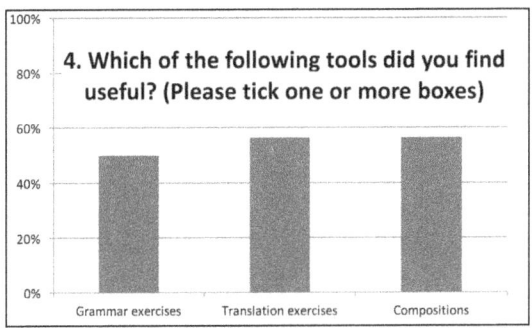

The analysis of these findings shows that while grammar exercises are appreciated by students who prefer a formal and structured approach to language learning, the writing tasks ('compositions') are preferred by those who see culture as a way of learning a second language.

Students' comments on the grammar exercises[3] show students' awareness that certain grammatical constructions may not receive sufficient practice during the

---

3. Question 4B; https://research-publishing.box.com/s/cihuzkz5v5k71k0511ghrqj1v8snr76e

YA and that consolidating knowledge of morphology and syntax in a short time span is a challenge inherent to the Italian beginners programme[4].

3. Discussion

3.1. Analysis

The views expressed by students are in line with larger studies showing that explicitly learned rules of morpho-syntax require longer time than lexical forms to be automatised (VanPatten, 1996, p. 30).

Writing compositions on cultural topics is a way of transferring knowledge of Italian culture into the study of language and of seeing cultural and linguistic competences as part of the same coherent project. The QAA Benchmark Statements of 2015, which define what can be expected of a language graduate at the end of their studies, strongly promotes this view:

> "The study of languages enables students to understand the similarities and differences between cultures, in the broadest sense of high culture, popular culture and the customs and practices of everyday life. In this sense it is inherently intercultural" (QAA, 2015, point 2.2).

The responses to the questionnaire confirm that different students have different learning styles. Language tutors also need to acknowledge this and give students the opportunity to enhance their language skills through different means. The translation appeals to those students who like reflecting on the differences between two languages[5].

Studies on translation as a way of reflecting on morpho-syntactic features (Cook, 2010; George, 1972) demonstrate how this task allows learners to

---

4. See responses to Question 5; https://research-publishing.box.com/s/cihuzkz5v5k71k0511ghrqj1v8snr76e

5. See responses to Question 5; https://research-publishing.box.com/s/cihuzkz5v5k71k0511ghrqj1v8snr76e

observe not only specific characteristics of the target language, but also observe the correspondence between target language features and their mother tongue equivalents. One student's comment also highlights the importance of using corrections on a written task to improve oral skills. Freed (1995) notes that investment in grammar instruction in the early stages of instruction may result in advances in speaking and listening at the upper intermediate and advanced levels.

Experience suggests that students will only engage with resources if the content is meaningful to them. In this particular context, students can relate the WLW to their existing knowledge of the language. They also understand its usefulness for future progress. This understanding is necessary for the students to respond well to the online resource as well as to independent learning in general.

The students' general feedback on the resource[6], allowed us to understand how they engaged with it. Their comments show a general concern about the lack of progress in writing skills during the YA and an understanding that regular use of WLW can help to improve the situation.

3.2. Measurable outcomes

Although data suggest there has been an improvement in the grades achieved by final-year students in their language exams since the introduction of the WLW, it would be risky to claim that the improvement is directly correlated to the WLW. Too many variables affect students' performances during tests, for example attitude to study and natural predisposition to L2 learning. However, we expect that regular use of the resource will help avoid fossilisation of errors and that this will have a positive impact on the performance in final-year language exams.

Figure 5 shows students' scores in the grammar exercises, in which 59.4% of the respondents' scores are in Class I. This is a positive result since most of the

---

6. See responses to Question 8; https://research-publishing.box.com/s/cihuzkz5v5k71k0511ghrqj1v8snr76e

grammar topics in the WLW are very challenging: use of gerund, translation of '-ing forms' in Italian, forms and use of the subjunctive, and the sequence of tenses within 'if clauses'. However, evidence that students can use these forms accurately would be provided only by an in-depth analysis of their language production.

Finally, it would be interesting to evaluate whether the WLW improved language performance in a communicative context. VanPatten's (1996, 2002) investigations show that advanced learners with a wider vocabulary and more control over grammar pay attention to grammatical forms even in a communicative context. A student commented as follows: "the corrections made me rephrase the way in which I said things in daily conversation". This subjective evidence is in line with VanPatten's (1996, 2002) studies and is an aspect of the WLW that deserves further investigation.

Figure 5. Grades achieved in grammar exercises

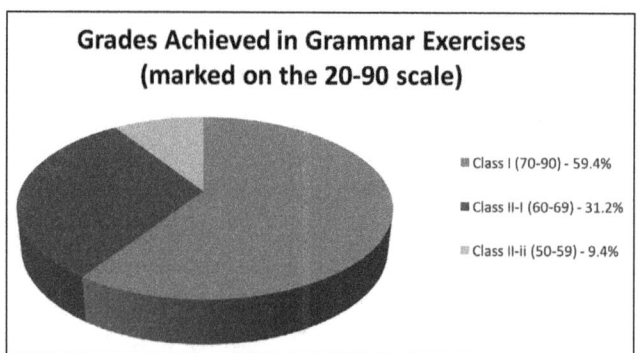

4. Conclusion

One of the outcomes at present is student satisfaction, indicated in responses to the questionnaire. In general, most students feel that the materials provided have helped them to reinforce morpho-syntactic structures and increase their ability to learn autonomously.

The SA experience offers tutors an opportunity to use independent and computer-based learning to create materials aimed at consolidating language competence and facilitating the process of second language acquisition, even at a distance. However, these materials need to be related both to the specific context of students' SA *and* to the taught programme. In addition, this study has shown that students are more likely to engage with independent and computer-based learning if the connection between independent learning and taught programme is clear to them and if they perceive the learning outcomes as relevant to their needs.

References

Batstone, R. (2002). Contexts of engagement: a discourse perspective on 'intake' and 'pushed output. *System, 30*(1), 1-14. https://doi.org/10.1016/S0346-251X(01)00055-0

Collentine, J. (2009). Study abroad research: findings, implications, and future directions. In M. Long & C. Doughty (Eds), *The handbook of language teaching* (pp. 218-233). Blackwell Publishing Ltd. https://doi.org/10.1002/9781444315783.ch13

Cook, G. (2010). *Translation in language teaching: an argument for reassessment*. Oxford University Press.

Freed, B. (Ed.). (1995). *Second language acquisition in a study abroad context*. John Benjamins. https://doi.org/10.1075/sibil.9

George, H. V. (1972). *Common errors in language learning: insights from English*. Newbury House.

QAA. (2015). *Subject benchmark statement – languages, cultures and societies.* http://www.qaa.ac.uk/en/Publications/Documents/SBS-consultation-Languages-Cultures-Societies-15.pdf

Stern, H. H. (1964). The future of modern languages in the universities. *Modern Languages, 45*(3), 87-97.

VanPatten, B. (1996). *Input processing and grammar instruction*. Ablex.

VanPatten, B. (2002). Processing instruction: an update. *Language Learning, 52*(4), 755-803. https://doi.org/10.1111/1467-9922.00203

4. Using online tools and resources to encourage independent learning amongst ab initio students of Italian: a case study

Paola Celant[1]

Abstract

This article describes the innovations introduced into the undergraduate *ab initio* Italian language programme at the School of Languages at the University of Bristol and the use of a range of online tools and resources. It evaluates to what extent the innovations have enhanced the students' experience. The article describes the course structure and how technology has been embedded in it. It looks at the pedagogy underpinning the choice of tools, explains how these tools are being used, and finally examines students' responses to the changes.

Keywords: blended learning, technology in the classroom, foreign languages, peer collaboration, learner autonomy.

1. Introduction

1.1. Description of the course

In common with Italian undergraduate courses at other UK higher education institutions, Bristol has two pathways: an *ab initio* pathway and a post-A-level pathway. *Ab initio* students are absolute beginners or near beginners in Italian.

---

1. University of Bristol, Bristol, United Kingdom; p.celant@bristol.ac.uk

How to cite this chapter: Celant, P. (2018). Using online tools and resources to encourage independent learning amongst ab initio students of Italian: a case study. In R. Biasini & A. Proudfoot (Eds), *Using digital resources to enhance language learning – case studies in Italian* (pp. 29-41). Research-publishing.net. https://doi.org/10.14705/rpnet.2018.24.796

Chapter 4

The course is intensive: in one year, learners are expected to reach level B1 of the Common European Framework of Reference for languages (CEFR).

First year *ab initio* students of Italian at the University of Bristol had five contact hours of language per week. Classroom-based learning consisted of one hour dedicated to oral and aural skills and four hours dedicated to integrated elements including grammar, reading, and writing (including translation). Student numbers vary from 15 to 25 per group (8-12 in the oral/aural class).

1.2. The need for change

About three years ago the Department of Italian decided to make changes to the first year *ab initio* course. The aim was to enhance the learning experience and engage students, at the same time making full use of the new, purpose-built MultiMedia Centre (MMC) with its wide range of multimedia resources and the strong support network offered by the University's Technology Enhanced Learning (TEL) team.

We wanted to draw on the principles of blended learning which, "with the combination of synchronous verbal and asynchronous written communication in the context of a cohesive community of inquiry, […] offers a distinct advantage in supporting higher levels of learning through critical discourse and reflective thinking" (Garrison & Kanuka, 2004, p. 98).

1.3. What we did

The teaching team introduced a one-hour weekly computer laboratory session in the MMC. The five hours per week of classroom based learning now consist of:

- one hour of oral and aural skills in small groups;

- three hours of integrated skills in a traditional classroom setting; and

- one hour in the computer laboratory in the MMC.

The teaching team devised a range of online resources to use during the MMC session. These included *Sanako*, a virtual language laboratory; *Mediasite*, a video platform; *Questionmark Perception*, an online testing tool; and *Blackboard*, the Virtual Learning Environment (VLE). The activities created with these tools and resources can be used outside the MMC for students' independent learning. The activities are described in detail below.

2. Methodology

2.1. Rationale

In planning the changes to the *ab initio* course, the tutors focussed on using a range of multimedia resources in order to promote: (1) exposure to the target language, (2) social interaction and collaborative learning, and (3) learner autonomy.

2.1.1. Exposure to the target language

Learning a new language is easier when it takes place in the target country. Students cannot easily do that in the first year at university, therefore technology was used to bring the outside world into the classroom. Exposure to the target language can be maximised by the use of technology: students have "access to native speakers [... and] easy 24/7 access to [...] instructional and authentic language learning materials" (Lai & Gu, 2011, p. 317).

2.1.2. Social interaction and collaborative learning

According to Egbert and Hanson-Smith (1999), in their study of computer assisted language learning, optimal language learning conditions will be achieved when "learners interact in the target language with an authentic audience" and when "learners are involved in authentic tasks" (p. 4). Social constructivism promotes the idea that "learning occurs not only individually but also through social interaction" (Nakata, 2006, p. 118). This approach "stresses the need for a collaborative learning environment where learners are enabled and encouraged to interact with and support one another, a public space characterised by interaction and collaboration" (Schwienhorst, 2007, p. 19). A way had to be found to create this interaction and authenticity of environment and tasks in the new MMC hour.

2.1.3. Learner autonomy

According to Egbert and Hanson-Smith (1999), learner autonomy is another of the ideal conditions for effective language learning. Autonomy is the learners' ability to critically reflect on their own learning, to communicate and collaborate with other learners, and to take control and assume responsibility for their own learning (Schwienhorst, 2007). Students have to be guided and encouraged to take charge of their own learning.

The 24/7 availability of the VLE and online resources, and a clear structure to guide them through, assists students keen to develop their language skills further via independent learning, helping them to test themselves and to take control of their own learning.

2.2. Computer assisted class activities: the MMC hour

To introduce these innovations, we used a blend of university managed software and online tools:

- *Blackboard*, as a VLE;

- *Sanako*[2], a language learning software available in the computer suite;

- *Questionmark Perception*, a dedicated system for delivering and managing online formative and summative assessment and examinations; and

---

2. http://www.sanako.com/en-gb/products/study-1200/

- *Mediasite*[3], the university's centrally supported enterprise video platform.

Each weekly class in the MMC uses a range of tools, according to its aims and objectives.

2.2.1. Blackboard

Blackboard is used for all the components of the *ab initio* Italian course: it provides separate sections for reading skills, oral classes, the MMC hour, etc., and is easy to access and navigate. *Blackboard* is widely used as a VLE across the university, so is familiar to students.

In the MMC hour, *Blackboard* is the starting point for most class activities. Each week all material is made available on a specific area of the *ab initio* Italian *Blackboard* module, to which students can refer to outside of class.

Wherever possible, students are given authentic tasks, accessing Italian websites that Italians might use, for example, carrying out their online weekly shopping in an Italian supermarket[4], ordering take-away food[5] or searching for a new house on an Italian estate agents' website[6]. After the research, students write up their findings (individually or in pairs) in a blog or wiki, shared with the rest of the class. Usually, work started in class is completed at home, where students can still collaborate without needing to be in the same room.

Students then give general feedback to their peers, commenting on the content (opinions on the chosen menu/house/etc.) rather than the language. Students' work is generally corrected but not awarded marks. Students also use *Blackboard*'s wiki and blog tools to create short stories based either on visual elements (such as short

---

3. http://www.bristol.ac.uk/tel/support/tools/mediasite/
4. http://www.sunmarket.it/
5. http://www.justeat.it/domicilio/italiano/roma/
6. http://www.agenzieimmobiliari.com/

videos, publicity material, or pictures) or on written stimuli, and to work together on translation tasks. Again, all this work is corrected but not formally assessed.

2.2.2. Sanako

Sanako is a multimedia language lab software with classroom management. It is a modern version of the old language lab which allows students to get more involved in the lesson and to actively participate in all language learning exercises. Each weekly class in the MMC generally starts with a vocabulary test created via the learning software *Sanako* and delivered to students individually. Upon logging onto their computers, students are presented with word lists in Italian or English which they need to translate within a given amount of time. The test ends automatically when the set time is over; the tutor is able to check all scores and answers before sharing individual results with each student.

Another main function of *Sanako* used in class is the text chat facility. This is used in two ways, both individually and in small groups.

> (1) Working individually, students access an online chat room via their computer and type a response to, or comment on, a stimulus launched online by the tutor: either a warm-up activity or a vocabulary revision activity. By typing their responses or comments in the chat room, everyone can contribute synchronously, including students who are normally shy or reluctant. The general atmosphere becomes quickly relaxed and playful, great for breaking the ice and reducing the stress typically associated with "foreign language anxiety" (Horwitz, Horwitz, & Cope, 1986, pp. 125-132).

> (2) Working in pairs or in groups, students work collaboratively on a more structured task. This can be a written conversation in the form of text chat targeting a particular language point (e.g. organising an informal date or a formal meeting using modal verbs) or for general communication skills (e.g. ordering a meal, etc.). Students work in pairs

or in groups of three and collaborate and help each other in writing their messages, thus creating a dynamic interactive exchange. The tutor can observe and intervene discreetly from the main computer station while students enjoy the variety of tasks.

2.2.3. Questionmark Perception

Language assessment in the first year includes various components, two of which (grammar tests) are delivered online via *Questionmark Perception*, which is an online testing tool used to design, create, and deliver formative and summative online assessment. The Department of Italian has successfully used this tool to create grammar tests and exams for several years. Activities created include multiple choice, matching, fill in the gap, and true/false. Although creating tests can be time consuming, the material can be re-used repeatedly.

Short formative grammar tests distributed throughout the academic year help students learn and revise, and familiarise them with the test format in advance of the two summative tests (labelled 'End of Teaching Block One and Two'). Formative tests are introduced in class as a 10-15 minute activity during the MMC hour, and subsequently made available online.

2.2.4. Mediasite

As already mentioned, the programme has a strong focus on independent learning: students are expected to spend at least five hours per week working independently (and a further five hours per week on homework). They are free to choose how they do this.

Another innovation aimed at encouraging independent learning was the introduction of an online library of video grammar tutorials. *Mediasite* allows the creation, editing, and publishing of material (via *Blackboard*) and management of content. Two *ab initio* tutors used the *Mediasite* tool to create twenty-six short video grammar tutorials (8-12 minutes each) to accompany PowerPoint presentations previously used in class: one video per grammar point. The video tutorials become available online after each class. These recordings are not intended as an alternative to attending class but rather as a revision tool freeing up class time for other activities.

From the tutors' point of view, it has been a positive experience: any initial reluctance about video recording oneself quickly disappeared, thanks to the enthusiastic response from the students. In terms of time constraints, while the first year has been relatively demanding for the tutors making the recordings, the same material can be reused in the future. From the students' point of view, as illustrated later, this has been a great success.

3. Evaluation

Several data sources were used to evaluate the innovations: a printed survey[7], an online survey (see Table 1), *Mediasite*'s video analytics, and built-in reports on Blackboard (see Figure 1).

Table 1. Online survey (May 2016)

1. I have enjoyed the lessons in the Multimedia Centre (MMC): 1 2 3 4 5 *
2. Classes were well structured: 1 2 3 4 5 *
3. Classes were interactive and interesting: 1 2 3 4 5 *
4. I felt motivated by being in the MMC: 1 2 3 4 5 *
5. I feel my language knowledge has been reinforced: 1 2 3 4 5 *
6. I feel I have learned what I was supposed to: 1 2 3 4 5 *
7. I would have preferred a more traditional approach (no computers, classroom based) : 1 2 3 4 5 *
8. What was the best element about these classes? And the worst?
9. I found all technology in the MMC classes easy to use: 1 2 3 4 5 *
10. I feel I had enough instructions from my tutor: 1 2 3 4 5 *
11. I find my IT skills have improved: 1 2 3 4 5 *
12. Which of the following activities/tools did you find useful? : A B C D E **
13. Which of the following did you find particularly enjoyable and/or stimulating? : A B C D E **

---

7. https://research-publishing.box.com/s/0o8rj375xam3hiem5k958s4sr1m9qak4

14. What do you think could be improved and/or changed in the MMC classes?
15. Any further comments?
* 1. Strongly Agree; 2. Agree; 3. Neutral; 4. Disagree; 5. Strongly Disagree ** A. Vocabulary test B. Group chat activities C. Wiki/blog for creative writing D. Wiki/blog for translation E. Online grammar tests

Figure 1. Mediasite analytics: example

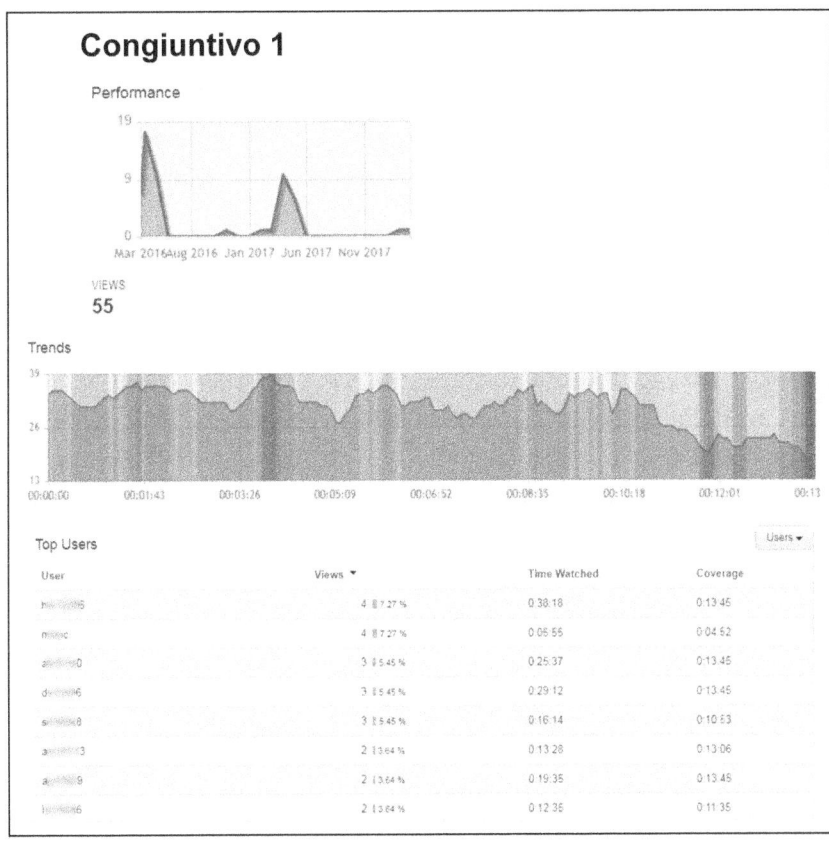

The printed survey was a standard end of year 'language unit evaluation questionnaire' commissioned by the School of Modern Languages. It included questions on the entire language course including its components, the use of *Blackboard*, and the online material available for independent learning.

The online survey, on the other hand, was created specifically this year by the Italian Department to gather students' opinions on the way the MMC teaching room was used. It included 15 questions, of which three were open questions inviting comments on the positive and negative elements of the MMC hour and on how to improve it. The rest were closed questions, evaluating various aspects of the classes and the resources used.

At the end of the academic year, students were asked to complete both surveys. Out of the 43 students in the *ab initio* language course, 34 completed the printed survey, 32 of whom also completed the online survey. All responses were anonymous. The aim was to identify both positive and negative perceptions of the use of IT, both in class and outside the classroom, and produce recommendations for ways to improve the materials and students' engagement with the material.

Finally, *Blackboard* allows tutors to access information on the use students make of the *Mediasite* tutorials. Each video tutorial contains video analytics and built-in reports which allow tutors to identify students' engagement and behaviour, with intensity maps indicating which video segments are watched most or least (Video Analytics, 2017).

4. Results

The overall feedback for the MMC hour and its related activities was very positive.

The Language Unit Evaluation Questionnaires generally showed appreciation for all aspects of the *ab initio* course. There was a particularly enthusiastic response to the video grammar tutorials: at least 50% of the 34 completed questionnaires contained a positive comment on the *Mediasite* material, such as "video tutorials were AMAZING", "loved the grammar tutorials", and "the grammar tutorials allowed me to go over things if I didn't understand".

Mediasite's video analytics confirm this enthusiasm: students accessed the video tutorials fairly regularly but the peaks in usage correspond to the days following class explanation and the revision period preceding tests and exams.

More information on the use of the computer laboratory and of technology was gathered from the online survey. As stated earlier, 32 out of 43 students completed this questionnaire. Over 84% of respondents enjoyed the lessons in the MMC and found them interactive and interesting, while 81% felt that their language knowledge had been reinforced. A small percentage of students (12%) would have preferred a more traditional approach, without the use of computers.

Overall, the positive comments outnumbered the negative ones. In their comments, learners stated that they enjoyed the relaxed and stimulating atmosphere and felt that the use of technology helped their learning: "it feels like a more relaxed class, lots of discussion between my peers"; "the use of computers, etc. is very useful for language-learning, it helps to establish resources that we can use at home, and breaks up the week, so that not everything is classroom-based, which may have been a bit dry" (online survey).

Generally, students appreciated the variety of tasks, the level of creativity involved, and the exposure to authentic Italian resources and culture. They also enjoyed the collaborative side of these classes, remarking: "the best part was being able to work together in a more relaxed way and be able to improve in ways that would have been hard without using the computers" (online survey).

The comments on specific online activities were again very positive: "I liked the vocabulary tests on the computer [...] as you can check your mistakes soon after the test", "vocab test every week was motivating", "loved when we used the chat facilities on *Sanako*", "online grammar tests is [sic] good practice to put to use what we have learnt in the other classes" (online survey).

In two cases, however, learners felt that for some activities the use of computers was superfluous: "I felt, for a lot of the exercises we did in class, using computers to do them was unnecessary – they could easily have been done on paper, and if that were the case I would have found them easier to focus on", and "I feel at times technology wasn't used effectively and we could have done the same material in the MMC that we do in normal classrooms, without the added distraction of computers" (online survey). Negative responses on the use of computers occurred seven times in the online survey: five students disliked the technical issues linked to computer use and two found computers an extra source of distraction. Moreover, one student felt that unless work was "officially marked" by the tutor, "it was difficult to be motivated enough to complete [...] tasks started in the lessons" (online survey).

5. Conclusion

This paper presented an overview of the way in which online tools were introduced into the *ab initio* Italian language course. The aim of the initiative was to use the principles of blended learning to enhance the learning experience, making it dynamic, engaging, effective, and interactive. A carefully planned blend of online tools was integrated with a weekly lesson in the MMC and with students' independent learning.

As learners' comments have shown, integrating new technology into the course has been beneficial to their learning process and level of engagement; it has enabled the teaching team to cater for all learning styles and needs, both inside and outside the classroom, and has made lessons generally more enjoyable and motivating.

Although the response from students was largely positive, it is clear that a small minority of learners see the use of computers in class as an obstacle rather than facilitating the learning process. A clearer explanation of the aims and objectives of the initiative might help all learners to appreciate the use of technology in the classroom and motivate them further.

References

Egbert, J., & Hanson-Smith, E. (Eds). (1999). *CALL environments: research, practice, and critical issues*. Teachers of English to Speakers of Other Languages, Inc.

Garrison, D. R., & Kanuka, H. (2004). Blended learning: uncovering its transformative potential in higher education. *Internet and Higher Education, 7*(2), 95-105. https://doi.org/10.1016/j.iheduc.2004.02.001

Horwitz, E. K., Horwitz, M. B., & Cope, J. (1986). Foreign language classroom anxiety. *The Modern Language Journal, 70*(2), 125-132. https://doi.org/10.1111/j.1540-4781.1986.tb05256.x

Lai, C., & Gu, M. (2011). Self-regulated out-of-class language learning with technology. *Computer Assisted Language Learning, 24*(4), 317-335. https://doi.org/10.1080/09588221.2011.568417

Nakata, Y. (2006). *Motivation and experience in foreign language learning*. Peter Lang.

Schwienhorst, K. (2007). *Learner autonomy and CALL environments*. Routledge.

Video Analytics. (2017). http://www.sonicfoundry.com/mediasite/manage/analytics/

5. ITALO (MyLearning Log): a case study in the use of technology-based resources to foster student engagement and autonomy

Salvatore Campisi[1]

Abstract

This paper describes the project 'ITALO (MyLearning Log)', introduced as part of the Institution-Wide Language Programme (IWLP) at the University of Manchester. The project aimed to encourage student engagement with the Virtual Learning Environment (VLE), monitor usage and effectiveness of the resources deployed, and develop learner autonomy. Three elements were central to the project: the resources on Blackboard, the tutors, and examples of good practice from former students. Learners tried out and commented on online resources, and shared their findings and best practice in a learning log, thereby also helping the tutor monitor learners' progress. The paper first describes the background to the project and the rationale behind it. It then describes the project in detail and the methods used to evaluate the results. An analysis of the key findings shows how the project has benefited current students. Finally, in the conclusion, we evaluate the success of the project and discuss the potential for further research.

Keywords: student engagement, technology-based resources, learning community, learner autonomy.

---

1. University of Manchester, Manchester, United Kingdom; salvatore.campisi@manchester.ac.uk

How to cite this chapter: Campisi, S. (2018). ITALO (MyLearning Log): a case study in the use of technology-based resources to foster student engagement and autonomy. In R. Biasini & A. Proudfoot (Eds), *Using digital resources to enhance language learning – case studies in Italian* (pp. 43-53). Research-publishing.net. https://doi.org/10.14705/rpnet.2018.24.797

© 2018 Salvatore Campisi (CC BY)

Chapter 5

1. Introduction

The project 'ITALO (MyLearning Log)' was developed as part of the IWLP at the University of Manchester and piloted with three groups of students from the Italian beginners' module in the academic year 2014-2015. The project was then refined and extended to the Italian pre-intermediate group the following academic year.

The project's primary aim was to address poor student engagement with the resources available on Blackboard, the institutional VLE. Previous end-of-year student evaluations of IWLP courses showed that students did not believe the resources available online significantly enhanced their learning. The ITALO project sought to monitor usage and effectiveness of resources deployed on the VLE and encourage learner autonomy.

Three elements were identified as central to the project: the resources on Blackboard, the tutors, and examples of good practice from former students.

Resources were grouped in categories, and students were free to explore them independently[2]. The tutor, however, played an active role in "[co-opting] the student into the learning process, encouraging active participation in their own development" (Berdrow & Evers, 2011, p. 407). Testimonials from previous learners, who had distinguished themselves for their extensive use of resources on Blackboard, provided further incentive and guidance for students.

In the second iteration of ITALO (2015-2016), special emphasis was placed on interaction and exchange of information among users, pivotal components of autonomy, in line with recent scholarly findings: "the development of autonomy necessarily implies collaboration and interdependence" (Benson, 2001, p. 12)[3].

---

2. Resources were grouped under two main headings, 'Materials prepared by tutors' and 'External resources', which included: 'Generic language websites for Italian', 'Grammar and revision', 'Vocabulary and pronunciation', 'Radio, TV, and newspapers', and 'Music, hobbies, and tourism'.

3. See also Ivanovska (2015, p. 353) on the value of interdependence for the development of autonomy.

ITALO was therefore a resource-based project, which combined two of the approaches to independent learning: directed independent learning, "in which students are guided by curriculum content, pedagogy and assessment, and supported by staff and the learning environment, and in which students play an active role in their learning experience" (Thomas, Jones, & Ottaway, 2015, p. 4), and the e-learning community, "where a group of learners communicate and share knowledge with each other with the assistance of an e-moderator" (Sloman & Reynolds, 2003, p. 261).

To monitor usage and effectiveness of the VLE resources, learners were asked to keep a 'learning log' (using the Blackboard journal tool), where they would record their exploration of the VLE and their learning strategies. The dual purpose of the journal was therefore to contribute towards student engagement with Blackboard and indirectly provide feedback to tutors on the resources.

Together with the independent exploration of the VLE resources and the sharing of knowledge via the learning logs, we used questions to attract students to the resources available on Blackboard and to prompt an inquiring and therefore more autonomous attitude to the learning process[4].

2. Methodology

Of the three key components of ITALO (resources, tutors, and testimonials), the testimonials required longer elaboration, as they were central in arousing curiosity in students about Blackboard resources and triggering thoughts on the learning process. We opted to have three short videos, where two former beginner students, who had achieved a high level of linguistic competence as well as learner autonomy, answered three key questions on how they had developed as independent learners: (1) 'What kind of resources do you use on Blackboard for learning Italian and why?', (2) 'Which resources would you recommend to study Italian outside class and why?', and (3) 'What tips would

---

4. Reflection and questioning are important in the development of an autonomous learner: "Self-directed learning means learners engaging in inquiry. Inquiry means getting answers to questions" (Knowles, 1975, p. 99).

Chapter 5

you give students to help them learn independently?'. The three video clips were posted on a dedicated section of the VLE, and students were asked to watch them at the beginning of the course before starting their own exploration of the existing materials and resources on Blackboard (Figure 1).

Figure 1. ITALO's starting page with introductory videos

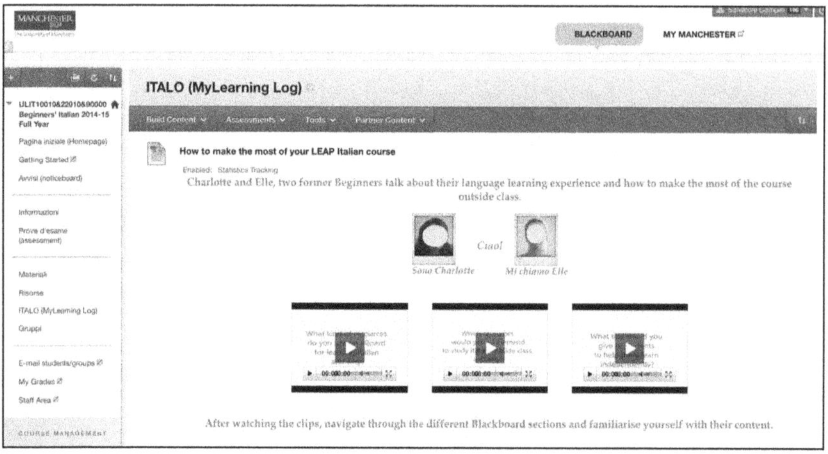

After the first three-four weeks of lessons (9-12 hours of instruction), students were invited to reflect on their learning progress and periodically (at least three times per semester) record their reflections in their individual journal (ITALO, MyLearning Log). They were asked to outline their achievements, difficulties, ways in which they had overcome a learning problem, and the resources they used (Figure 2). Students could type their entries into their journal, add audio/video recordings or, alternatively, link their journal to a Padlet (https://padlet.com/), a virtual noticeboard where multimedia content can easily be added.

The learning logs were not assessed; however, students were strongly encouraged to take part in the exercise, as an integral part of the learning process. During the first year of implementation (2014-2015), journals were kept 'private' (students could view only their own entries), to avoid self-comparison with peers and the risk that learners might feel intimidated by their fellow students' scrutiny. The following year, however, tutors took the decision to trial the logs in 'public' mode so that users could view and comment on their peers' entries.

Figure 2. Outline of the project and its objectives for students

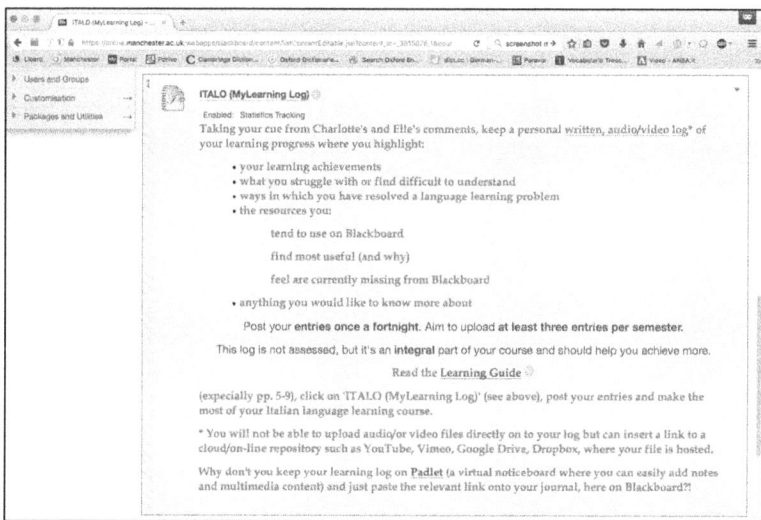

Tutors reviewed students' entries halfway through the semester, collated those which appeared most innovative or effective, and showed them in class as a means of giving feedback to those who had participated, encouraging those who had not, and disseminating examples of good practice. The role of the tutor was therefore to facilitate the exchange of information, especially during the first year when journals were 'private', and motivate students. Journals also provided tutors with valuable feedback on the users' learning progress and on the overall effectiveness of the resources deployed on the VLE.

Given ITALO's practical focus on student engagement, we concentrated our attention on student participation and journal contributions in our evaluation of the project outcomes, leaving other forms of evaluation such as eliciting student views on the project or on learner autonomy for later iterations of the project.

3. Results and discussion

Despite the initial uncertainty over student engagement, as learning logs were not going to be formally assessed, students positively responded to ITALO as an opportunity to exploit the VLE to its full potential and maximise their learning opportunities. Half the students across the three groups of beginners contributed posts to their learning log during the year the project was piloted, and two-fifths actively participated the following year (see Table 1). Students tended to contribute more during the first semester, when they were still becoming familiar with the course and the resources available on the VLE[5]. Although these numbers may not suggest a high participation rate, they are in fact very positive, as all e-learning communities typically include a number of 'lurkers'; "people who are willing to read […] messages and documents but not to make contributions" (Sloman & Reynolds, 2003, p. 270)[6].

All ITALO contributors chose to type posts in their learning log, occasionally adding hyperlinks to resources located outside the VLE. None opted for audio/video entries or the use of Padlet.

Table 1. Number and length of student contributions per year

	No. of students (3 groups)	Contributors (total)	Contributions (total)	No. of words (total)	No. of words per contriutor (average)
2014-15	28	14	22	2655	190
2015-16	47	20	41	7459	373

Most users broke down their reflections into sections, whose main headings were often the points they were asked to consider before starting their log (learning

---

5. There is also a further factor to take into account, a natural decline in motivation in the second semester, when students may easily feel "tired of keeping the learning log" (Hu & Zhang, 2017, p. 154) or perceive the exercise as "too time consuming" (Coomey & Stephenson, 2001, p. 39).

6. This definition draws on Gilly Salmon's investigation of 'lurking' in online learning (Salmon, 2011, see especially pp. 175-178).

achievements, ongoing difficulties, solved problems, and resources used; see Figure 3), and only a few adopted a more discursive, diary-style approach, generally signalled by the informal tone of their opening line (e.g. "Greetings all, I thought I'd let people know what online resources I've found useful").

Figure 3. Student entry with personal learning achievements, difficulties, and resources used on Blackboard

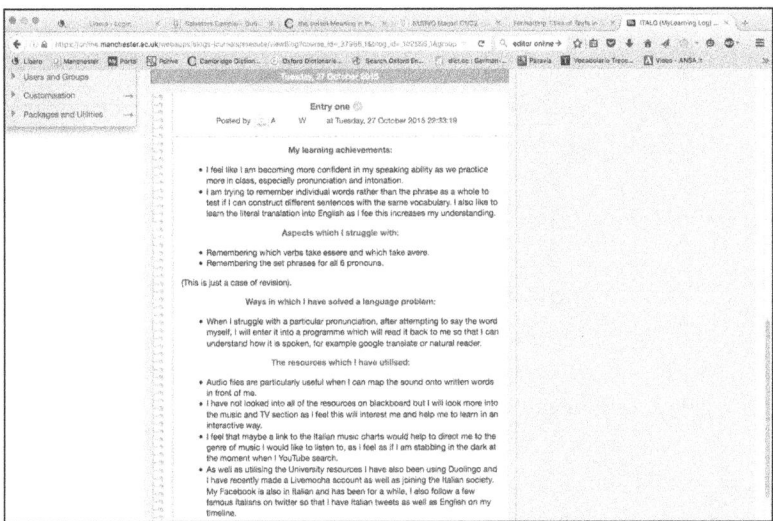

The data and insights into students' learning processes that ITALO posts have provided can be broadly divided into four categories: (1) learning strategies, (2) learning difficulties, (3) use of resources, and (4) instances of interaction and collaboration[7]. In many cases, entries provided information on more than one category at the same time, as shown by some of the examples in the remaining part of this section. Learning strategies ranged from traditional ones ("I have coloured stickers around the house to remind me of the words, and I try to rehearse them when I am out and about"), to those aided by technology ("setting

---

7. The four categories resonate with Mynard's (2012) analysis of student blogs in her case study, where entries showed evidence of 'critical reflection', 'metacognition', 'decision-making', and 'problem-solving (p. 6). Indeed, ITALO students evaluated and recommended resources, assessed how they learnt best, indicated reasons for using given tools or strategies, and explained how they had overcome a learning problem.

Chapter 5

my phone to Italian is weird at first but it does help with keeping me in the mindset"). The entries have also pointed to students' preferred learning styles:

> "tried to learn the numbers better. I did this by watching videos on YouTube… I feel like it helped a lot more than just looking at a sheet of paper!".

Students have also described their stumbling blocks:

> "So far I mostly struggle to remove an 'English' frame of mind when writing Italian. Getting used to saying 'the my parents' took some time, though through much practice it's becoming […] easier".

Other entries have indicated how learners have solved a learning problem:

> "When I struggle with a particular pronunciation, after attempting to say the word myself, I will enter it into a programme which will read it back to me so that I can understand how it is spoken, for example google translate or natural reader".

The use students have made of the VLE resources has brought their learning strategies to the fore too:

> "Everyday I spend ten minutes on Memrise learning Italian vocab, ten minutes on DuoLingo doing the same thing, ten minutes on an app like Padlet called MentalCase to learn verbs and then around five minutes on an app called Lingualy".

In some cases, users have extensively reviewed the resources they tried (see Figure 4). Although students have not replied to their peers' posts with comments, even when journals were 'public', ITALO contributions show clear evidence of collaboration and cross-fertilisation among its users: "I watched Peppa Pig in Italian on YouTube after seeing it on someone else's ITALO log", and "I have discovered the addictive world of Quizlet! Am sharing folders with [A.] and [C.]".

Figure 4. Student entry evaluating resources available on Blackboard

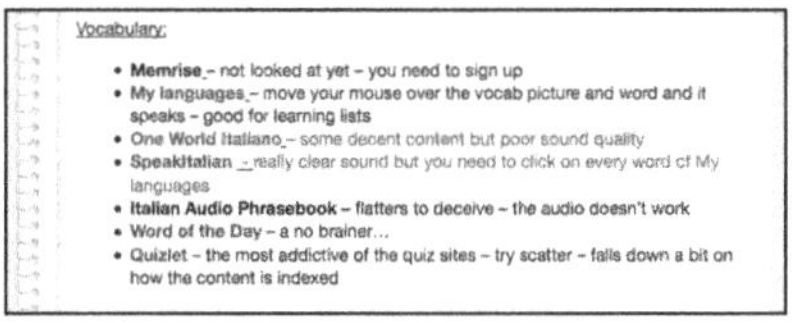

> Vocabulary:
> - **Memrise** – not looked at yet – you need to sign up
> - **My languages** – move your mouse over the vocab picture and word and it speaks – good for learning lists
> - **One World Italiano** – some decent content but poor sound quality
> - **SpeakItalian** – really clear sound but you need to click on every word of My languages
> - **Italian Audio Phrasebook** – flatters to deceive – the audio doesn't work
> - **Word of the Day** – a no brainer…
> - **Quizlet** – the most addictive of the quiz sites – try scatter – falls down a bit on how the content is indexed

4. Conclusion

The project has evolved and improved over the past two years. Fewer students contributed posts during the second year: 20 out of 47 compared to 14 out of 28 in 2014-2015 (see Table 1). The average number of entries per contributor, however, increased from 1.59 in 2014-2015 to 2.05 the following year, and the average number of words each contributor wrote almost doubled. Moreover, entries in the second year were generally more structured and substantial than those appearing in 2014-2015 (see Figure 3). The project has undergone refinements since its initial trial. Capitalising on the first year's pilot, tutors were able to guide students with more targeted interventions and examples; for instance, selected entries from the previous year were visible to users while they were writing their posts. Moreover, making the journals 'public' has encouraged interaction, making the VLE a learning community rather than just a repository of resources.

In future research, it would be useful to: engage in a quantitative analysis of Blackboard real-time usage reports to measure the impact of the project on overall student engagement with the VLE; assess the effect of ITALO on student linguistic attainment and final grades by involving only two groups and using the third group as a control; and investigate the learners' perspective on ITALO and its influence on their attitudes to independent learning, with questionnaires administered at the end of the academic year.

The design of ITALO reflects the latest evolution of CALL, "the integrative phase […] characterised by the use of multimedia, hypermedia and interactive technologies to promote integration of skills" (Benson, 2001, p. 138). It displays instances of the "four major features of online learning widely identified as essential to good practice[:] dialogue, involvement, support, control" (Coomey & Stephenson, 2001, p. 38)[8], and has promoted "autonomy [by taking] learners beyond the provision of their teachers and [engaging] with a greater variety of materials, learners, [and] support tools" (Coomey & Stephenson, 2001, p. 49).

Acknowledgements

I would like to thank the students who contributed to ITALO and who gave permission for the publication of extracts from their online journals. I would also like to acknowledge the key role of my colleagues, Maria Kluczek (senior language tutor in Italian) and Helen Perkins (e-learning technologist), who initiated the project, and Maria's assistance with this paper. The detailed comments and advice given by reviewers have been greatly appreciated.

References

Benson, P. (2001). *Teaching and researching autonomy in language learning*. Pearson Education.

Berdrow, I., & Evers, F. T. (2011). Bases of competence: a framework for facilitating reflective learner-centered educational environments. *Journal of Management Education, 35*(3), 406-427. https://doi.org/10.1177/1052562909358976

Coomey, M., & Stephenson, J. (2001). *Online learning: it is all about dialogue, involvement, support and control – according to the research*. http://www.academia.edu/2028329/Online_learning_It_is_all_about_dialogue_involvement_support_and_control-according_to_the_research

Hu, P., & Zhang, J. (2017). A pathway to learner autonomy: a self-determination theory perspective. *Asia Pacific Education Review, 18*(1), 147-157. https://doi.org/10.1007/s12564-016-9468-z

---

8. The learner independently explores the VLE resources in ITALO (control) and can interact with other users (dialogue), whereas tutors encourage active participation (involvement) and monitor and direct exchanges (support).

Ivanovska, B. (2015). Learner autonomy in foreign language education and in cultural context. *Procedia - Social and Behavioral Sciences, 180*(1), 352-356.

Knowles, M. (1975). *Self-directed learning: a guide for learners and teachers*. Association Press.

Mynard, J. (2012). Raising awareness of learning processes with technology tools. *Proceedings of the Technology in the Classroom 2012 Conference*, Osaka (1-9). http://www.academia.edu/2861764/Raising_Awareness_of_Learning_Processes_with_Technology_Tools

Salmon, G. (2011). *E-moderating: the key to teaching and learning on-line* (3rd ed.). Routledge.

Sloman, M., & Reynolds, J. (2003). Developing the e-learning community. *Human Resource Development International, 6*(2), 259-272. https://doi.org/10.1080/13678860210155412

Thomas, L., Jones, R., & Ottaway, J. (2015). Effective practice in the design of directed independent learning opportunities. *The Higher Education Academy, Quality Assurance Agency*, 1-69. https://www.heacademy.ac.uk/sites/default/files/resources/effective_practice_in_the_design_of_directed_independent_learning_opportunities.pdf

6. The Italian electronic language log: a critical evaluation

Simone Lomartire[1]

Abstract

The present article focusses on the use of the Electronic Language Log (ELL) as a tool to monitor independent learning practices by *ab initio* students of Italian in their first year of study at the University of Leeds. The ELL is first described in the pedagogic framework from which it derives, the language log; the primary aim of this contribution, however, is to give a direct analysis and critical evaluation of the work produced by students for their ELL and, specifically, of the work submitted in the academic year 2015-2016. Key findings show how this learning tool has helped beginner students of Italian manage their own learning independently. Emphasis is placed on students as the primary owners of the ELL and on their preferences for self-directed, mobile-learning (m-learning) practices. The conclusion discusses the potential of the ELL for evaluating students' skills and competences in Italian, and whether the ELL is fulfilling its purpose effectively.

Keywords: electronic language log, m-learning, self-directed language learning, language apps, online technology.

---

1. University of Leeds, Leeds, United Kingdom; s.lomartire@leeds.ac.uk

How to cite this chapter: Lomartire, S. (2018). The Italian electronic language log: a critical evaluation. In R. Biasini & A. Proudfoot (Eds), *Using digital resources to enhance language learning – case studies in Italian* (pp. 55-65). Research-publishing.net. https://doi.org/10.14705/rpnet.2018.24.798

Chapter 6

1. Introduction

1.1. The language log

The language log is a tool for learning widely employed in language classes in Higher Education Institutions (HEIs) in the UK to record independent language learning practices (Kühn & Pérez Cavana, 2012; López-Fernández, 2014). It has two objectives: the development of learner autonomy and the recording of language activities, ranging from written texts, drawings, and student reflections to audio or video recordings. The language log is also regarded as a flexible tool where student work done outside the classroom can be stored (Kühn & Pérez Cavana, 2012; Trappes-Lomax & Ferguson, 2002)[2].

1.2. The electronic language log at the University of Leeds

The Italian department at Leeds adopted the language log in 2009 as a record of independent learning for first and second year students; since 2012 it has taken the form of an ELL[3], which is an electronic Word document which students submit online at the end of each semester.

In the first-year *ab initio* programme, the ELL is the major component of students' independent work, helping students record what they have done by submitting screengrabs. *Ab initio* students of Italian have four hours per week contact time over a ten week semester (in both Semesters 1 and 2). Language progression has to be rapid: starting at the Common European Framework of Reference for Languages (CEFR) A1 in Semester 1, students must reach CEFR A2[4] at the end of the second semester of their first academic year. To ensure these levels are reached, students must engage in eight to ten hours a week of

---

2. For a concise yet meticulous summary of background literature on student autonomy, see Kristmanson, Lafargue, & Culligan (2013).

3. Electronic versions of the language log are becoming increasingly popular in the HEI context due to the advantages of the digital configuration; these have been effectively summarised by a recent article by Ciesielkiewicz & Méndez Coca (2013).

4. A1 corresponds to the first while A2 to the second level on a six-level scale of competence laid down in the CEFR. For more on the CEFR scale, see the eponymous publication by the Council of Europe's (2017) Language Policy Unit.

self-directed study, 70% of which must be devoted to the ELL[5], which they start to build in Semester 1. ELL carries ten percent of the final mark for the two core language modules, one in Semester 1 and one in Semester 2.

Students are offered guidance on compiling their ELL: at least ten tasks per skill, per semester, should be included and students are given a list, with brief descriptions, of online language resources available for free – mostly podcasts, video channels, e-books, and language apps – which they are encouraged to use and record in their own log. The resources complement the classroom teaching which makes extensive use of communicative language teaching[6] and are intended to consolidate the four basic language skills in the context of the chosen task. Upon task completion, students are asked to paste a screengrab into the ELL, uploading the file to a designated area of the relevant Italian language module, on the Virtual Learning Environment (VLE). Students are given the option of organising the screengrabs in the document by date, tutorial, skill, or language function.

Even though students can choose from an array of free resources, since the implementation of the ELL most have concentrated on app-based tasks alone. Screengrabs have included tasks from *Duolingo*[7], *Memrise*[8], *Lingua.ly*[9], and *Linqapp*[10]. *Duolingo* focusses on morphological and syntactical elements matching the CEFR A1 and A2 descriptors for Italian but also alternates between reading, speaking, listening, and writing tasks. *Memrise* and *Lingua.ly*, as flashcard generator apps, make use of "mems" and *ad-hoc* flashcards respectively, which consist of associative visuals for A1 and A2 high-frequency Italian words, phrases, or longer texts aimed at enhancing short- and long-term

---

5. The remainder of this time is devoted to the completion of a separate workbook.

6. Particularly, communicative language teaching approaches which stem from integrated models of facilitation and humanistic models (Biggs & Tang, 2011; Bosisio, 2005; Bosisio & Chini, 2014; Mezzadri, 2015; Richards & Rodgers, 1986; Tarone & Yule, 1989).

7. http://www.duolingo.com

8. https://www.memrise.com/

9. https://lingua.ly

10. http://www.linqapp.com

memory skills and vocabulary. Additionally, *Lingua.ly* relies on a solid corpus of Italian texts from various online sources – whether tweets, blogs, or newspaper articles – where key vocabulary can be learnt in context, and virtually any word from any text can instantly be converted to a flashcard. *Linqapp* consolidates students' speaking skills by engaging them in simple conversations at A1 and A2 level.

The ELL at Leeds emerged from the development of mobile and online technology[11]. While still promoting self-directed learning, as did the paper-based language log, it does so primarily through m-learning[12]. The ELL allows learners to piece together the different artefacts, "in a single location, organised chronologically, thematically, or according to a specific purpose" (Cummins & Davesne, 2009, p. 849). It is also simpler to update and access the ELL since "all the information that it contains can be downloaded [and consulted remotely] in order to be carefully studied and researched" (Ciesielkiewicz & Méndez Coca, 2013, p. 465). Finally, the tasks in the ELL can be stored for future reference (Kristmanson, Lafargue, & Culligan, 2013).

2. Methodology

The aim of the present study is to investigate how the ELL was used by first-year *ab initio* university students of Italian and evaluate its effectiveness as a tool for independent learning. The study adopted qualitative methods to analyse students' use of the ELL and their preferred independent learning practices while evaluating how such practices impacted on students' involvement in the language learning process.

The analysis was carried out at the end of the academic year 2015-2016 by assessing 60 logs produced by 30 first-year students (the average size cohort). Feedback from students was also elicited via the university module

---

11. For a detailed classification of pedagogic uses of mobile and online technology, see Patten, Sánchez, & Tagney (2006).
12. For a comprehensive study on m-learning, see Herrington et al. (2009).

questionnaires which are distributed at the end of every taught module. Only answers from questionnaires distributed at the end of the core language module in semester two were considered in this analysis to ensure a balanced perception of students' independent learning habits and use of the ELL throughout their entire first year of study at university. The answers to two specific questions provided the basis of our results: (1) 'What was the best thing about the module?'; and (2) 'In addition to the prescribed reading for the module, what have you done to get the most out of the module?'. Students were asked to incorporate ELL-specific comments in their answers to these module-wide questions.

3. Results

The analysis of the ELLs and of the screengrabs included provides insights into students' independent language study habits. The results demonstrate an extensive range of language tasks and a marked preference for m-learning, mostly app-based tasks. This is backed up by students' comments in the module questionnaires.

The four language apps with the most screengrabs were: *Duolingo* (60 logs), *Linqapp* (60 logs), *Memrise* (46 logs), and *Lingua.ly* (28 logs). *Duolingo* is predominantly used by students for translations of simple sentences from English to Italian and transcription of short spoken sentences in Italian. Judging from the frequency with which these tasks appear in students' ELLs, the app plays a significant part in their independent learning. In the questionnaires, the majority (95%) also mentioned *Duolingo*'s translations where the tasks fit well with the summative exams for Level 1 Italian (notably the written and listening test). Sixty percent of students also commented favourably on *Duolingo*'s rapid-fire quizzes which are mostly used to consolidate their independent learning but also to compete against fellow students in the same group[13].

---

13. For more on the rationale behind this, see the section in Duolingo's home page (http://www.duolingo.com/).

Chapter 6

Memrise and Lingua.ly are mostly selected by students for vocabulary-building exercises and monitoring both reading and pronunciation. Screengrabs of *Memrise* show that the majority of students create their own "mems" either by taking pictures of relevant items or by selecting photos from a portfolio of google images which reflect key vocabulary covered in the set textbook in class (36 logs); a minority of students use the app to draw their own flashcards (10 logs). Seventy percent of students also found the "mems" a helpful revision tool as the app sends regular reminders to test the same word or phrase, a popular feature as students approach the end of their module and their exams.

A few students also use *Lingua.ly* to revise their vocabulary through purpose-made flashcards independently; at least six logs were filled with screengrabs of such flashcards. However, *Lingua.ly* is primarily used to show engagement with longer texts in Italian and key vocabulary in context; this explains the greater popularity of this app with A2 rather than A1 students. Indeed, screengrabs of the chosen text and its related flashcard were found mostly at A2 level (20 logs at A2 versus only two logs at A1 level).

Many students (46%) also commented positively on *Lingua.ly* in the questionnaires, particularly on the way the app 'invites' them to create a corpus of texts based upon their reading habits[14]. This allows students to assimilate key vocabulary in context, combined with a set of review sessions, with the added bonus that the Italian words are presented as a network of synonyms rather than a series of disconnected words.

The remaining screengrab evidence provided by students in their ELL relates to their speaking practice outside the classroom using *Linqapp*. All the A1 users presented screengrabs of forum chats with other native Italian speaker *Linqapp* users; frequent discussion topics include simple points of grammar for clarification, but also cultural questions. At A2 level, students took screengrabs of conversations which took place via VoIP[15] with native Italian speakers, using

---

14. The app gathers information on students' reading habits and suggests other written pieces, similar in content and length.
15. The app is built-in with a VoIP system to communicate among users.

Linqapp, creating a genuine language exchange, with occasional questions on Italian linguistics.

Among the positive aspects of *Linqapp* mentioned in the questionnaires was the sense of community generated by interactions with other language learners (40%). Students (78%) also enjoyed using *Linqapp* to upload photos of street signs, food menus, and extracts from written texts for other users to comment on[16].

4. Discussion

From my review of students' work produced for their ELL, it became clear that a number of common practices emerged in the ways Level 1 beginner students of Italian used the ELL to gather evidence of their independent study. These focused on action-oriented language tasks, as advocated in the CEFR (Council of Europe, 2017), and included:

- a preference for vocabulary-building exercises by means of kinaesthetic activities, from the creation of flashcards with the most commonly used Italian words to word games;

- grammar and/or translation activities used as a means to develop language skills to communicate, with a prevalence of exercises based on integrated skills (such as written comprehension questions on an aural text);

- the need for regular testing and revision;

- the desire to interact with a native speaker, in order to communicate and work as part of a community of learners.

---

16. Linqapp facilitates such exchanges through a points system: according to the complexity of the comment given, users gather points which allow them to gain an "experienced status" within the Lingapp community – something many students appear to value as part of their log.

Chapter 6

These findings further demonstrate how students, in selecting the tasks they want to carry out, make their own choices, demonstrating individual learning styles, whilst at the same time being motivated to work in groups or to support other app users. Specifically, while *Duolingo* gives students the chance to work together outside the classroom, *Linqapp* offers students the opportunity to work with a community of individuals from the most diverse backgrounds who are just as interested in learning as they are in helping one another, with the added bonus that students are also exposed to other languages.

Concurrently, my observations seem to confirm what has been posited by Ciesielkiewicz and Méndez Coca (2013), i.e. that the ELL appears to be a flexible tool to monitor students' independent learning. It is also easier for students to update their ELL as screengrab evidence can be added easily and students can use their logs to look back on their learning journey at the end of both semesters through the screengrabs. In particular, as revealed by the questionnaires, for 98 % of students their ELL often turns into a reliable language companion (Cummins & Davesne, 2009).

However, independent learning practices identified in the ELL also carry a number of constraints. Some language apps are more appropriate to certain CEFR levels than others. *Duolingo* does not teach the pragmatic competences needed for both second- and final-year students, while *Linqapp* may offer too intense a learning experience for A1 students. It is clear then that app-based tasks should be used in conjunction with one another and that the four independent study habits referred to above should not be seen as mutually exclusive.

At a different level, external pressures, which challenge both the format of the ELL and the validity of the app-based tasks, also exist. Ever since its initial implementation, the ELL has been met with some resistance among the less technologically literate users, and not only among them[17]. A more discerning approach to technology-enhanced learning is sometimes adopted both by

---

17. Debate in this sense is still ongoing. Solid and informed reflections are offered by Hart and Hart Frejd (2013), Cummins (2007), and Gibson (2006, pp. 135-145).

students and by some facilitators who lament both the effects of "education based technology" (Hart & Hart Frejd, 2013, p. 46) and the sometimes intrusive nature of apps such as *Memrise*. Universities also tend to put emphasis on their own VLE. These VLE platforms frequently come with their own language and online tools for independent learning, thereby competing with the language apps discussed here.

5. Conclusion

While the ELL may vary from one institution to another, this study can help us draw conclusions on how this tool can be employed to assess students' independent learning and how examples of good practice can be extended to other languages as well. The study has shown that, in spite of the obstacles preventing its full implementation, the ELL offers an effective complementary tool to monitor independent language learning habits within HEIs, especially for *ab initio* students of Italian in their first year of study. The ELL appears to be successful in recording students' achievements and experiences. Importantly, the flexibility and adaptability of the tasks can accommodate different learning styles, responding to students' individual learning needs.

Concurrently, students not only seem aware of the learning goals they want to reach through their choice of app-based tasks for the ELL, but they also seem aware of the potential of their self-directed learning practices, while their curiosity seems to be stimulated by the app-based tasks chosen independently. In this way, students ultimately achieve what Kohonen (2004) called "invisible learning outcomes", i.e. those goals that "are essential for the development of language competence and student autonomy" (p. 32).

References

Biggs, J., & Tang, C. (2011). *Teaching for quality learning at university*. McGraw-Hill and Open University Press.

Bosisio, C. (2005). *Dagli approcci tradizionali al quadro comune europeo di riferimento.* EDUCatt.

Bosisio, C., & Chini, M. (2014). *Fondamenti di glottodidattica.* Carocci.

Ciesielkiewicz, M., & Méndez Coca, D. (Eds) (2013). The electronic language portfolio as a tool for lifelong learning. Proceedings from *ICT for Language Learning* – 6th *Conference Edition, Florence.*

Council of Europe. (2017). *Common european framework of reference for languages: learning, teaching, assessment.* Language Policy Unit.

Cummins, P. (2007). LinguaFolio and electronic language portfolios in teacher training. In M. A. Kassen, R. Z. Levine, K Murphy-Judy & M. Peter (Eds.), *Preparing and developing technology- proficient L2 teachers* (pp. 321-344). CALICO Monograph Series 6. Computer Assisted Language Instruction Consortium.

Cummins, P., & Davesne, C. (2009). Using electronic portfolios for second language assessment. *The Modern Language Journal, 93*, 848-861. https://doi.org/10.1111/j.1540-4781.2009.00977.x

Gibson, D. (2006). ePortfolio decisions and dilemmas. In A. Jafari & C. Kaufman (Eds.), *Handbook of re-search on e-portfolios* (pp. 135-145). Idea Group.

Hart, D., & Hart Frejd, S. (2013). *The digital invasion – how technology is shaping you and your relationships.* Baker Books.

Herrington, J., Herrington, A., Mantei, J., Olney, I., & Ferry, B. (Eds). (2009). *New technologies, new pedagogies: mobile learning in higher education.* University of Wollongong.

Kohonen, V. (2004). On the pedagogical significance of the European language portfolio: findings of the Finnish pilot project. In K. Mäkinen, P. Kaikkonen & V. Kohonen (Eds.), *Future perspectives in foreign language education* (pp. 27-44). Studies of the Faculty of Education of the University of Oulu 101.

Kristmanson, P., Lafargue, C., & Culligan, K. (2013). Experiences with autonomy: learners' voices on language learning. *The Canadian Modern Language Review/La revue canadienne des langues vivantes, 69*(4), 462-486. https://doi.org/10.3138/cmlr.1723.462

Kühn, B., & Pérez Cavana, M. L. (2012). *Perspectives from the European language portfolio.* Routledge.

López-Fernández, O. (2014). University teaching experience with the electronic European language portfolio: an innovation for the promotion of plurilingualism and interculturality. *Cultura y Educación, 26*(1), 211-225. https://doi.org/10.1080/11356405.2014.908667

Mezzadri, M. (2015). *I nuovi ferri del mestiere.* Loescher.

Patten, B., Sánchez, I., & Tagney, B. (2006). Designing collaborative, constructionist and contextual applications for handheld devices. *Computers in Education, 46*, 294-308. https://doi.org/10.1016/j.compedu.2005.11.011

Richards J., & Rodgers T. (1986). *Approaches and methods in language teaching.* Cambridge University Press.

Tarone, E., & Yule, G. (1989). *Focus on the language learner: approaches to identifying and meeting the needs of second language learners.* Oxford University Press.

Trappes-Lomax, H. R., & Ferguson, G. (2002). *Language in language teacher education.* John Benjamins Publishing Company. https://doi.org/10.1075/lllt.4

7. Using, adapting, and sharing learning resources to widen participation in language learning: a case study of Italian open educational resources for dyslexic students

Anna Motzo[1]

Abstract

The learning difficulty known as dyslexia affects up to ten per cent of the adult population. In current teaching practice in Higher Education Institutions (HEIs), however, there is still little awareness of how dyslexia-friendly language course materials can be created. Language learning materials, although often delivered in novel digital formats, show little evidence that new dyslexia-friendly approaches have been considered. It is suggested that this lacuna presents a challenge to language departments in HEIs and requires the provision of dedicated teacher training. This case study offers an insight from the perspective of the practitioner on how to use, re-use, and adapt existing language learning materials in ways that are designed to improve the learning experience for dyslexic learners and benefit non-dyslexic learners at the same time. The author illustrates how a set of existing Italian language Open Educational Resources (OERs) were modified and/or created by adopting a Multisensory Structured Language (MSL) approach which combines visual, auditory, kinaesthetic, and tactile pathways and utilises the structuring/re-patterning of the way information is presented and colour coding of the visual field, in order to help improve learner attention, retention, and processing of information.

Keywords: OERs, widening participation, dyslexia, multisensory language approach.

---

1. The Open University, Milton Keynes, United Kingdom; a.motzo@open.ac.uk

How to cite this chapter: Motzo, A. (2018). Using, adapting, and sharing learning resources to widen participation in language learning: a case study of Italian open educational resources for dyslexic students. In R. Biasini & A. Proudfoot (Eds), *Using digital resources to enhance language learning – case studies in Italian* (pp. 67-79). Research-publishing.net. https://doi.org/10.14705/rpnet.2018.24.799

Chapter 7

1. Introduction

Addressing learners' differing needs and styles is a key aspect of any teaching practice aimed at successfully promoting an inclusive learning environment, which fosters and widens learner participation. This is particularly relevant in a distance/online learning environment where learners need to be able to study autonomously and independently.

The Open University (OU) has been offering courses in modern languages for over 20 years.

The languages currently on offer for OU undergraduate students (Chinese, French, German, Italian, and Spanish) are delivered using blended learning, which comprises a mix of both instructor-led sessions (face-to-face and online) and self-study. The OU's core learning material, which is created in-house, constitutes an essential aspect of the learning experience which is carefully designed to help learners develop their language skills, while also fostering the development of their autonomy and metacognitive skills.

Almost two percent of the OU language learners have declared themselves to be dyslexic; the actual percentage however might be higher, given that some learners have never been screened[2].

In 2013, the OU's School of Languages and Applied Linguistics (formerly 'Department of Languages') ran the Dyslexia Modern Language Learning (DMLL) scholarship initiative, which aimed to create a repository of knowledge on the topic of dyslexia and language teaching and learning – see Motzo and Quattrocchi (2015) for an account of the DMLL project. As an output of the project, a number of OERs for teaching and guidelines for teachers were produced and made available in Languages Open Resources Online (LORO), the OU's online open source language repository (http://loro.open.ac.uk/).

---

2. Data provided by the OU information office and referred to academic years 2014-15 (2015-16 and 2016-17).

The present case study, following up from the DMLL scholarship project, reports on the author's attempt to provide some practical examples on how to create and repurpose language OERs that would cater for language learners with dyslexia or other learning difficulties.

2. Literature review

As mentioned in Gallardo, Heiser, Arias-McLaughlin, and Fayram (2013, p. 4), dyslexia is a processing difference which primarily affects reading, writing, and spelling, but can also impact on cognitive processes such as memory, processing speed, time management, coordination, and automaticity. There may be visual and/or phonological difficulties and there are usually some discrepancies in educational performances (Kormos, 2012; Reid, 2009).

Although there is not yet a conclusive and definitive etiology of dyslexia, the general consensus is that it is caused by a phonological processing deficit, resulting from neurological factors (Gabrieli, 2009). All agree that it comprises a wide spectrum of learning differences. In the clinical context, where it is studied in the light of the common discrepancy between high IQ and low performance, dyslexia is defined as a disorder, deficiency, disability, or abnormality. Following Kormos (2012), however, I have chosen to refer to it as a 'learning difference'. In other words, learners with dyslexia seem to have common traits in their preferred learning style and their skills-set, which include holistic and lateral thinking, spatial and visual thinking, problem-solving ability, and creativity.

Some pivotal studies (Fawcett & Nicolson, 2008) have indicated that in dyslexics information is processed differently due to the fact that in the dyslexic brain the right hemisphere, responsible for creativity and synthetic skills, seems to be more dominant than the left hemisphere, responsible for language acquisition and more analytical skills. It is crucial therefore for teachers and dyslexic learners not only to be aware of the characteristic features of dyslexia, but also to enhance those skills which are connected to the right hemisphere of the brain and which, if properly harnessed, can foster a positive learning experience. This is particularly relevant in the context of language learning and teaching, where on the one hand dyslexic learners may encounter difficulties in literacy skills, while on the other hand there is a tendency to structure linguistic activities in ways that are heavily reliant on cognitive functions (sequencing, structuring, abstraction, memorisation, and so on). Such functions are supported by the left hemisphere and little adjustment is made to address the needs and styles of dyslexic learners.

In the UK, around seven million people are affected by dyslexia (British Dyslexia Association, 2007; Dyslexia Action, 2009). This is ten percent of the whole population. It is also estimated that around four percent of the current Higher Education (HE) population is dyslexic[3]. However, taking into account that not all learners affected by dyslexia have been assessed or have disclosed their learning difficulty, the total number of HE learners with dyslexia might be higher than statistics would indicate.

Research also suggests that adopting an MSL approach, whereby a simultaneous combination of learning tools and stimuli is used through two or more of the four core sensory channels (hearing; saying; feeling; seeing) to enhance memory and learning of written language, has a considerable positive impact on language learners with dyslexia (Ganschow, Sparks, & Schneider, 1995).

Dyslexic learners often experience problems with visual processing or poor auditory memory or both, and therefore benefit from multisensory learning where connections between two or more sensory pathways are designed into the learning experience (Birsh, 2005; Fletcher, Lyon, Fuchs, & Barnes, 2007; Schupack & Wilson, 1997). Recently, there have been various publications aimed at promoting good teaching practice in developing or adapting dyslexia-friendly materials (Gallardo et al., 2013; Sánchez Gordón & Luján Mora, 2015).

Furthermore, in 2015, the first dyslexia and language teaching Massive Open Online Course (MOOC) from Lancaster University was launched on the FutureLearn platform.

---

3. https://www2.le.ac.uk/offices/accessability/staff/supporting-students-with-dyslexia/dyslexia_guidelines/dyslexia_he

3. The project

This case study reports on the DMLL project, described in the introduction, aimed at adapting and repurposing existing language OERs in order to support learners with dyslexia.

The resources described here were created by a team of two academics (the author and OU Associate Lecturer Sandra Silipo) using PowerPoint and Jing (https://www.techsmith.com/jing-tool.html) and were also saved as whiteboard files (.wbd) in order to also be used interactively and collaboratively in virtual classrooms via the Blackboard Collaborate teleconference software. PowerPoint is useful as slides can encompass objects in various formats (text, graphics, sound, videos) and allow a high degree of versatility; they can either be printed or used online. Jing is a screencast software which allows images or video to be captured and uploaded on the web.

In the next paragraph, four digital resources created for the OU will be discussed. All are compatible with both Mac and Windows and can be used with tablets or other digital devices.

Once created, all the OERs were reviewed by a Dyslexia & Disability Support expert who commented:

> "[The] sets I felt were clear in their intention. The only comment I would have is that a visual image often aids memory and that the use of colour should be distinct enough to be obvious when placed on the visual sketch pad" (Mary Smith, Head of School, Dyslexia & Support, City of Westminster College).

3.1. OER 1: auditory discrimination using visual and oral stimuli

Learners with dyslexia can encounter difficulties in phonological processing, meaning they find it challenging to discriminate sounds or pronounce polysyllabic words (the auditory magnocellular hypothesis, Stein & Talcott, 1999). Their poor phonological awareness may affect speech perception and speech production, resulting in a low level of accuracy and verbal processing speed. Research indicates that problems with sound discrimination might be related to weaker phonological short-term memory (Baddeley, 1996) which appears to affect retention of new words, sustained attention, and concentration (Snowling, 2008), all of which are likely to impact on language learning. However, recent studies (Kormos, 2012) have indicated that a step-by-step programme which relies on explicit teaching, repetition, guided and structured learning, and which uses a kinaesthetic approach as part of active learning might benefit dyslexic learners.

The resources shown in Figure 1 were adapted and repurposed from an existing German resource designed to introduce four sounds in German [ei], [ie], [eu] and [au] using colour coding in order to help the learner by segmenting spoken words into phonemes and converting these phonemes into letters or combinations of letters to help them (graphemes). It made use of images in order to anchor the sound to a visual aid and help students store the sounds in their visual sketchpad (Motzo & Quattrocchi, 2015).

Figure 1. Auditory discrimination activity using visual and oral stimuli

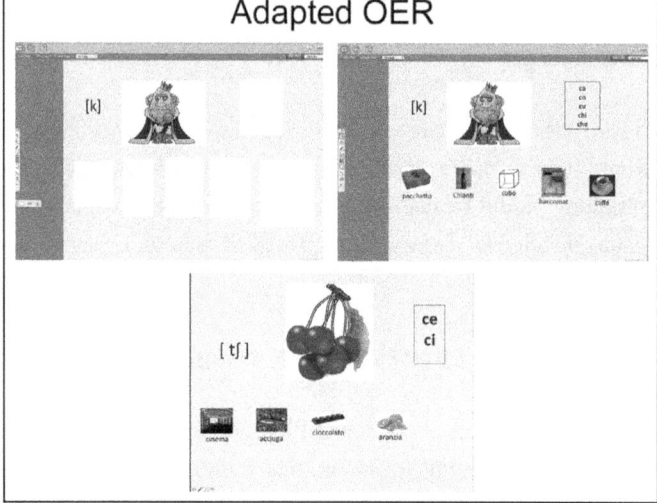

In Italian, the letter 'c' can represent various sounds depending on the letters it is combined with. 'C' can be sounded as either a guttural hard 'c' [K] as in English 'king', or a soft 'c' [tʃ] as in English 'cherry'. The two sounds may present further challenges when presented in written form (e.g. 'in English 'ch' is pronounced [tʃ]'), hence explicit teaching, mnemonic and visual aids, as well as ample scope for repetition are likely to help the process of sound recognition and eventually automatisation. The English equivalent spelling 'ch' was included with [tʃ] so that students have the visual and auditory correspondence of the English to the Italian spelling.

The resources were created in off-white as field studies indicate that dyslexic learners find it more difficult to read black on white backgrounds (visual magnocellular hypothesis, Martin & Lovegrove, 1987, also in Kormos, 2012).

The sound 'K' in Italian was introduced by anchoring it with a visual (image of a king) as well as the explicit information (word 'king') and making use of colour coding (red) to identify the relevant phoneme-grapheme mapping. In order to avoid overloading the page, the flashcards can be uncovered one by one so that learners can practise the sound [K] in its various combinations (co/ca/cu/chi/che) as shown in the next slide. When this sound was mastered, students could move to the sound [tʃ] following the same procedure. Extended activity included discriminating between the two sounds by listening and repeating them while looking at consistently used colour-coded labelled flashcards depicting words containing those sounds.

3.2. OER 2: understanding parts of speech through active learning and restructuring

Reading skills are developed on different hierarchical levels: word recognition through orthographic, phonological, semantic, and morpho-syntactic processing. It is by working across all these levels that readers achieve sentence comprehension and understanding of overall content. Vellutino (1979) pointed out that it is the phoneme to grapheme mapping that causes the most serious challenges for dyslexic learners when they read (phonological deficit hypothesis, Nicolson,

Chapter 7

Fawcett, & Dean, 2001). The lack of accurate mapping slows down reading and causes inaccurate word-recognition. Dyslexic learners with inadequate syllabic awareness will struggle in moving from the alphabetic to the orthographic stage, thereby compromising the reading process and understanding. It is hypothesised that they will benefit from exposure to overlearning using the MSL approach as well as explicit teaching and use of colour coding in order to move successfully to the next step of reading. One way to help the process of automatisation is to elicit visual memory (anchoring sounds and words to images) and episodic memory (contextual knowledge).

The OER illustrated below (Figure 2) was designed to help students reading a short simple text using visual aids, where kinesthesis and active learning help to elicit episodic memory in the process of automatisation. An effective MSL approach here would include reading the chunks aloud while moving them around in order to reorganise/re-sequence the text. This was found to be a particularly useful means of helping learners memorise communicative phrases and expressions.

Figure 2. An example of a modified and extended OER

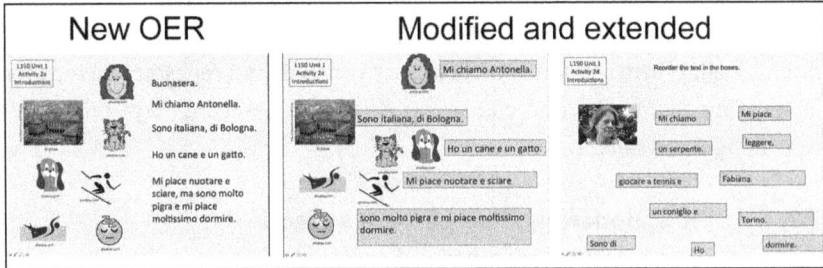

3.3. OER 3: examples of colour coded-based and kinaesthetic activities (word order rules)

Colour as an aid should be used with a specific intention and the learner should be aware of its significance. In this example of OERs for teaching possessive adjectives in Italian (Figure 3), some existing dyslexia-friendly OERs were modified to use colour coding consistently. As for all the OERs created, the background colour of the slides was changed and also the table was simplified to show only the singular forms of the possessive adjective. We cross-referenced the activity with the course materials (top left corner) and mapped nouns and adjectives applying the same colour coding (blue for masculine and green for feminine nouns and corresponding adjectives). The last slide shows an example of the extended interactive activity in which learners work on restricting word order by manipulation, moving from controlled to free practice.

Figure 3. An example of a colour-coded based and kinaesthetic activity (word order rules)

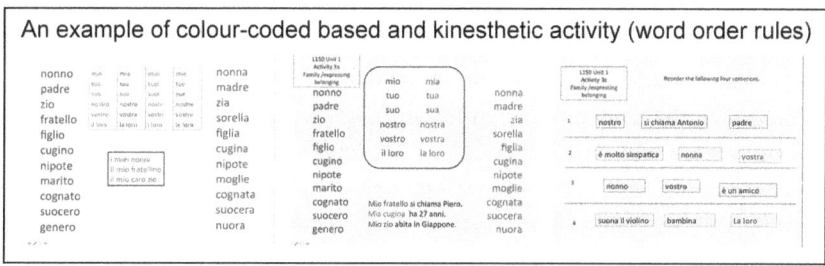

3.4. OER 4: understanding parts of speech

As in the previous example, the OER below (Figure 4) shows how multi-sensory techniques can also be applied in the teaching of grammatical structures. The colour coding of words or phrases that have different grammatical functions helps students understand grammatical concepts without using linguistic terminology (Kormos, 2012).

The visual shows how the original OER has been modified in order to use coding by font colours (red and blue) and style (bold) efficiently to provide learners with explicit teaching through a format of clear instructions supported by visual aids.

Figure 4. Adapted resource for part of speech

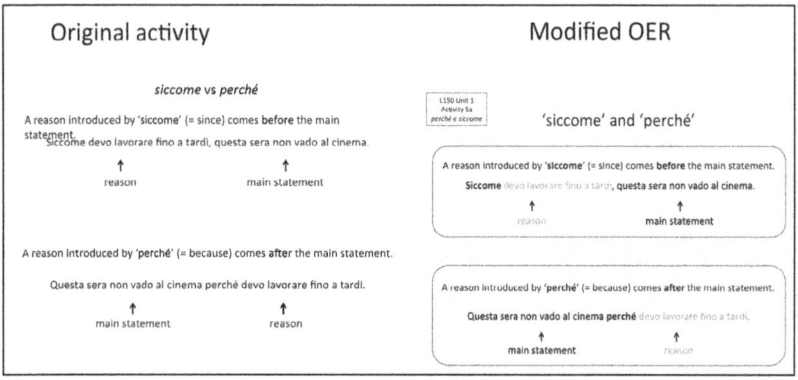

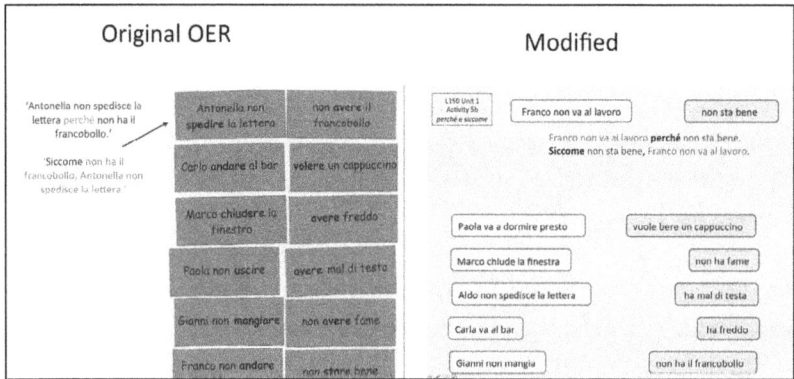

This final figure (Figure 5) shows how consistency and colour coding can be used to help learners perform more complex activities such as understanding parts of speech and restructuring. Here in the modified OERs, we simplified the task by adjusting the colour coding systematically (colour coding, off-white pastel colour background), teaching through modelling (example; cross-reference) and by changing the verb from infinitive to their correct finite form, given that the function of the activity was to work on causal sentences using connectors, rather than that of finding the correct verb form.

Figure 5. An example of the use of colour coding

4. Outcomes and limitations of the project

The set of OERs illustrates how language OERs were created, reused, and repurposed, using software such as Jing, PowerPoint, and Whiteboard, widely used in online learning and teaching, in order to address the needs and styles of dyslexic learners.

The examples described show how open educational resources can be adapted to enhance phonological awareness or facilitate reading skills hierarchy by imaginatively using the technological affordances of the selected software to promote an MSL approach.

The relevance and purposefulness of the resources were validated by informal feedback given by dyslexic learners, dyslexia support practitioners, and colleagues; any future development of the initiative, however, would require a comprehensive and systematic testing of the resources through formal feedback from dyslexic students.

5. Conclusion

This case study provides practical examples of how to create and repurpose open resources to widen participation in online language learning by addressing the needs and styles of learners with dyslexia. Based on recent studies, the author has defined dyslexia as a learning difference and has hypothesised that understanding the cognitive mechanisms of learning and subsequently adopting an MSL approach might support a positive learning experience for dyslexic learners.

Acknowledgements

Special thanks to Sandra Silipo (OU Associate Lecturer in Italian), who worked on adapting the learning materials, and Mary Smith, (Head of School, Dyslexia

& Support, City of Westminster College) for her invaluable feedback and comments on the efficacy of the resources adapted.

References

Baddeley, A. (1996). The central executive. *The Quarterly Journal of Experimental Psychology, 49*(1), 5-28. https://doi.org/10.1080/713755608

Birsh, J. R. (Ed.). (2005). Multisensory teaching of basic language skills. Paul H. Brookes Publishing Co.

British Dyslexia Association. (2007). *Dyslexia research information.* Reading: BDA. http://www.bdadyslexia.org.uk/

Dyslexia Action. (2009). *What is dyslexia.* www.dyslexiaaction.org.uk/

Fawcett, A., & Nicolson, R. (2008). *Dyslexia, learning, and the brain.* MIT Press.

Fletcher, J. M., Lyon, G. R., Fuchs, L. S., & Barnes, M. A. (2007). *Learning disabilities: from identification to intervention.* The Guilford Press.

Gabrieli, J. D. (2009). Dyslexia: a new synergy between education and cognitive neuroscience. *Science, 325*(5938), 280-283. https://doi.org/10.1126/science.1171999

Gallardo, M., Heiser, H., Arias-McLaughlin, X., & Fayram, J. (2013). *Supporting students with dyslexia in distance modern language studies. A guide to good practice.* http://loro.open.ac.uk/3912/

Ganschow, L., Sparks, R., & Schneider, E. (1995). *Learning a foreign language: challenges for students with language learning difficulties. Dyslexia-chichester-, 1,* 75-95.

Kormos, J. (2012). *Teaching languages to students with specific learning differences* (Vol. 8). Multilingual matters.

Martin, F., & Lovegrove, W. (1987). Flicker contrast sensitivity in normal and specifically disabled readers. *Perception, 16*(2), 215-221. https://doi.org/10.1068/p160215

Motzo, A., & Quattrocchi, D. (2015). Dyslexia in modern language learning: a case study on collaborative task-design for inclusive teaching and learning in an online context. In K. Borthwick, E. Corradini, & A. Dickens (Eds), *10 years of the LLAS elearning symposium: case studies in good practice* (pp. 89-102). Research-publishing.net. https://doi.org/10.14705/rpnet.2015.000270

Nicolson, R. I., Fawcett, A. J., & Dean, P. (2001). Developmental dyslexia: the cerebellar deficit hypothesis. Trends in neurosciences, 24(9), 508-511.

Reid, G. (Ed.). (2009). *The Routledge companion book of dyslexia*. Routledge.

Sánchez Gordón, S., & Luján Mora, S. (2015). Adaptive content presentation extension for open edX. Enhancing MOOCs accessibility for users with disabilities. *The Eighth International Conference on Advances in Computer-Human Interactions* (pp. 181-183).

Schupack, H., & Wilson, B. (1997). *The "R" book, reading, writing & spelling: the multisensory structured language approach*. The International Dyslexia Association.

Snowling, M. J. (2008). Specific disorders and broader phenotypes: the case of dyslexia. *The Quarterly Journal of Experimental Psychology, 61*(1), 142-156. https://doi.org/10.1080/17470210701508830

Stein, J., & Talcott, J. (1999). Impaired neuronal timing in developmental dyslexia—the magnocellular hypothesis. *Dyslexia, 5*(2), 59-77.

Vellutino, F. (1979). *Dyslexia: theory and research*. MIT Press.

Useful links

IDA. (2002, November 12). Fact sheet revised March 2008: http://www.interdys.org/ewebeditpro5/upload/AtRiskStudentsForeignLanguage2012.pdf

Dyslang: http://www.dyslang.eu/

Dyslexia in Higher Education, University of Leicester: http://www2.le.ac.uk/offices/accessability/staff/supporting-students-with-dyslexia/dyslexia_guidelines/dyslexia_he

OU DMLL Project The Guide to Good Practice: http://loro.open.ac.uk/3912/

8. Peer-teaching with technology: an Italian grammar case study

Marcella Oliviero[1] and Andrea Zhok[2]

Abstract

This case study centres on the notion that changing traditional student identities by turning them into 'student-teachers' can have very positive consequences on their involvement with the learning process. Technology plays a crucial role and is totally embedded in this approach. In this project, students are asked to research a grammar topic and generate tutorials using *Xerte* – an open-source authoring suite. They work collaboratively in small groups and teach their peers, delivering their own tutorials in class. Technology allows them to use a variety of techniques, texts and activities, which make the language learning process more creative and interactive. Support and supervision (both academic and technical) from tutors is available throughout the process. This method has proved highly motivating in terms of the acquisition and development of a wide range of transferable skills that go well beyond the specific learning objective – grammar revision – however central it may remain. The paper illustrates the project's background, rationale, planning, and workflow, and discusses our findings two years after implementation. It also evaluates its impact, effectiveness, and possible wider implications. While articulating a response to a local need for change, we aim at making this case study of interest to others and inspire in them a desire to innovate.

Keywords: peer-teaching, technology-enhanced learning, grammar, task-based learning, collaborative student-centred learning.

1. University of Bristol, Bristol, United Kingdom; mo12244@bris.ac.uk

2. University of Bristol, Bristol, United Kingdom; a.zhok@bris.ac.uk

How to cite this chapter: Oliviero, M., & Zhok, A. (2018). Peer-teaching with technology: an Italian grammar case study. In R. Biasini & A. Proudfoot (Eds), *Using digital resources to enhance language learning – case studies in Italian* (pp. 81-93). Research-publishing.net. https://doi.org/10.14705/rpnet.2018.24.800

© 2018 Marcella Oliviero and Andrea Zhok (CC BY)

Chapter 8

1. Introduction

This case study describes a project that was introduced in response to demands for change in a first year post-A level Italian language module for degree students and explains the context and the reasons why it was needed. This course is aimed at students with a British A-level diploma in Italian language or equivalent.

1.1. The educational context – the course

Students taking Italian at Bristol normally choose it as part of a joint honours degree in Modern Languages with another language (French, German, Spanish, Portuguese, or Russian). Other combinations include Italian with Drama, History of Art, Music, Philosophy, or Politics. A handful of candidates study Italian as a single honours programme.

The post-A level course at Bristol consists of three hours of tuition per week, divided into two blocks of eleven weeks over the academic session. This corresponds to the standard teaching provision in British universities (UCML Language Teaching Survey Report, 2014, pp. 4-5). One hour is dedicated to the formal learning of grammar and it is this component of the course which constitutes the focus of our project and is presented and discussed in this case study.

Classes typically consist of fifteen to twenty students, making up approximately a third of the department's annual intake. The remaining two-thirds are students taking Italian *ab initio*.

Although some students will have studied Italian for up to five years prior to joining the university, others might have taken an A-level as part of an accelerated course, while students taking A-level as individual candidates might never have studied grammar formally. These may include students from a native speaker background, e.g. heritage speakers. This is one of the reasons why the curriculum includes a complete revision programme, so as to give an equal grounding in the structures of the language to all students. By the end of the first year, students are expected to have reached a B1 level, according to the Common European Framework of Reference for Languages (CEFR).

1.2. The challenges

The post-A level unit had always posed certain challenges in the overall degree programme. Post-A level students and post-*ab initio* students merge in the second year at Bristol, but despite their perceived advantage, or possibly because of it and the misplaced sense of confidence it engenders, it was not uncommon to see post-A students fall behind post-*ab initio* students – a known phenomenon nationally (Worton, 2009). Better management of expectations regarding university study and the acquisition of stronger independent study skills in the transition from secondary to higher education were necessary. This, together with feedback from dissatisfied students, was an important driver for radical change.

Underpinning the course team's desire to innovate was the need to re-engage the students with the learning process and react positively to feelings of dissatisfaction amongst them. The idea of challenging them to teach each other seemed a suitable solution to prevent them from becoming passive and complacent about the subject matter.

1.3. A new grammar curriculum

A new teaching and learning approach necessitated a rethinking of the learning objectives. While the unit had mainly consisted of a rather traditional revision of grammatical rules, with the emphasis on morphology, drills, and limited sensitivity to context, the new programme would focus on the following aims:

- to provide a thorough and systematic revision of key grammar topics (from basic morphology to more advanced verb forms);

- to expose students to grammar in use in a wide range of contexts; and

- to emphasise the communicative purpose of grammar.

Moreover, the traditionally linear route from basic to more advanced topics was abandoned, in favour of a mix of easier topics alternating with more challenging ones from the very start, so that students would keep their focus high throughout the academic session, and avoid the impression that interesting topics would be addressed only towards the final stages of the course.

1.4. The project

Students are asked to research a grammar topic and generate tutorials using Xerte – an open-source authoring suite. They work collaboratively in small groups and teach their peers, each group delivering one tutorial in class per term. Technology allows them to use a variety of techniques, texts, and activities, which make the language learning process more creative and interactive. Support and supervision (both academic and technical) from tutors is available throughout the process.

The project is structured across several interlinked phases (see Figure 1).

Figure 1. Workflow chart

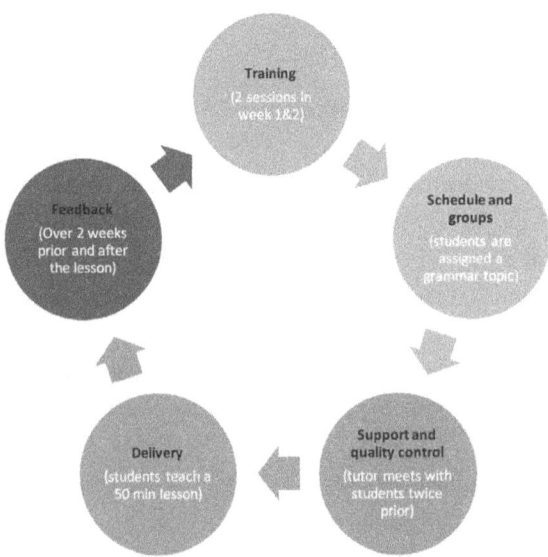

Firstly, students receive two IT training sessions in which they familiarise themselves with the tool and learn to use its functionalities. After students are divided into groups, assigned a topic, and given a delivery date for the lesson, two meetings are scheduled with the tutor (see Table 1).

The first meeting, two weeks prior to the delivery of the lesson, involves:

- an in-depth revision of the grammar topic; and
- an analysis of the lesson structure.

Each group is asked to think of a suitable context in which their grammar topic could be applied and to create a video in which they themselves perform.

Table 1. Detailed calendar of activities

Settimana	Gruppo	Studenti	Argomento	Appuntamento 1	Appuntamento 2
4	Gruppo 1	Harriet E. Isabella H. Camilla B.	Pronomi diretti	Mercoledì 8/10 Alle 12.30 (G107)	Lunedì 13/10 Alle 3pm (G107)
5	Gruppo 2	Barnaby B. Antonia L. Kalise P.	Pronomi indiretti	Lunedì 13/10 Alle 3.30pm (G107)	Lunedì 20/10 Alle 3pm (G107)
7	Gruppo 3	Elsa S. Olivia H. Giuliana Di R. Alice R.	Passato Prossimo VS Imperfetto	Lunedì 20/10 Alle 3.30pm (G107)	Lunedì 27/10 Alle 3pm (G107)
8	Gruppo 4	Victoria D. Samuel L. Christabel C. Tessa D.	Passato Prossimo VS Imperfetto	Lunedì 27/10 Alle 3.30pm (G107)	Lunedì 10/11 Alle 3pm (G107)
9	Gruppo 5	Eleonora R. Esme L. Benjamin F.	Pronomi relativi	Lunedì 10/11 Alle 3.30pm (G107)	Lunedì 17/11 Alle 3pm (G107)

Chapter 8

10	Gruppo 6	Joel D. Victoria E. Anne-Lise H.	Particelle CI e NE Verbi CONOSCERE e SAPERE	Lunedì 17/11 Alle 3.30pm (G107)	Lunedì 24/11 Alle 3pm (G107)
11	Gruppo 7	Leonora T. Isobel S. Chloe B.	Futuro	Lunedì 24/11 Alle 3.30pm (G107)	Lunedì 1/12 Alle 3pm (G107)

Students are asked to produce a lesson plan which includes:

- a short film to set the topic in a communicative context;

- the grammar explanation (following guidelines provided by tutor); and

- exercises and activities related to the topic.

Students are then given one week in which to complete their work. The second meeting, a week before the delivery of their lesson, aims to:

- check that the material produced by the students is appropriate (in terms of accuracy and with regards to the learning objectives);

- provide feedback on errors made; and

- provide advice on teaching strategies.

On the day of the lesson, students have fifty minutes in which to deliver their tutorial in the target language. 'Student-teachers' are advised to use a communicative approach, maintaining constant interaction with the 'student-learners'. This encourages students to work together to deduce grammar rules through questioning and helping each other. At the end of the lesson, the 'student-teachers' receive some final feedback from the tutor, evaluating their performance in terms of clarity, appropriateness, accuracy, and coherence.

2. Methodology

2.1. Pedagogic rationale and methods used

Turning students into agents of teaching as well as learning seemed to open an array of stimulating possibilities, especially when married to the idea of students as creators of digital learning tutorials, which would form the platform for their teaching. Jones (2007) goes even further, stating that:

> "students can't be 'taught' – they can only be helped to learn. In a student-centred classroom, our role is to help and encourage students to develop their skills, but without relinquishing our more traditional role as a source of information, advice, and knowledge. In a student-centred classroom, the teacher and the students are a team working together" (p. 25).

In this new environment, emphasis is placed on interaction between tutor, learners, and technology.

On a practical level, the tutor needs to plan the programme carefully in advance, so that students "are introduced to the technology and learning approach", at the same time, in line with the learning outcomes, "building in flexibility", in order to be ready to adapt to the learners' needs (Marsh, 2012).

The teacher becomes a facilitator, a coach, and 'guide on the side' (Jones, 2007), making sure that the topics are thoroughly understood by asking students questions, at the same time suggesting strategies and activities that might be effective in a specific lesson. Students are provided with 'scaffolding' and supported with presentation and teaching advice, but they have freedom of choice, for instance, as to what kind of exercises or activities they want to produce, the visual material they want to include, and the appropriate context for the lesson. The tutor motivates, encourages, and challenges students, questioning them in order to help them develop autonomy and reflect critically on their learning experience. Albeit behind the scenes, the teacher reviews the material produced, in order to guarantee its accuracy and effectiveness and to evaluate the students' progress. The result is a sharing environment in which input comes from both the students and tutor.

2.2. Choice of online tool

The online tool chosen for this project is the *Xerte Online Toolkit* (http://www.xerte.org.uk), an open source tool developed by the University of Nottingham and which became part of The Apereo Foundation initiative (https://www.apereo.org/) in 2014. It allows users to create interactive tutorials that incorporate texts, exercises, and other activities. It provides several interactive activity types such as gap fill, drag and drop activities, quizzes, and multiple choice exercises.

Furthermore, the tutorials can be enriched with pictures and audio-visual materials, relevant features which increase learner motivation, promote variety, and stimulate creativity. In addition, pages can be set up to provide explanatory feedback related to learners' responses. Consequently, the grammar lessons become more engaging and interactive.

Finally, Xerte was supported locally within our institution and was straightforward to embed into our local Virtual Learning Environment (VLE), supported by Blackboard, with positive implications for facilitating access to materials for independent study.

2.3. A change of learning dynamics

One of the most compelling consequences of flipping the learning experience and effecting it through a peer-teaching approach is the way in which dynamics change. In line with current structured constructivist pedagogy theories of peer-teaching and experiential learning (Falchikov, 2001; Whitman, 1988), our students' identities become more fluid and boundaries between tutor and learners more nuanced. Ownership and responsibility for the teaching and learning process undergo a shift, whereby teaching and learning become inextricably linked and can no longer be associated with one specific agent invested with a set of fixed expectations and roles – the tutor teaching, the student learning – such as in a more traditional pedagogic model.

One important aspect of this learning environment is the centrality that planning and design acquire. Students become active stakeholders in collaboratively designing their own learning experiences in line with Kress and Selander's (2012) concept of "interaction design" where "one not only focuses on products, but also on, for example, social processes at different workplaces, and emphasis is laid on the making of products" (p. 266).

This learning model, the environment it creates and the learning acts, exchanges, and objects (the digital tutorials authored by the students) which it facilitates, lead the students through the range of tiers of learning identified by Bloom's revised taxonomy, from remembering and understanding to applying, analysing, evaluating, and finally creating (Anderson & Krathwohl, 2001). Although not all tiers are equally developed, the higher tiers play a dominant role in our model.

2.4. Assessment

A change of pedagogy requires a realignment of assessment practices. While the summative aspect of assessment entails the grammar component being tested as part of the students' end of year written exam (through a series of contextualised grammar exercises modelled on and consistent with the topics and task types practised during the year), formative feedback during the entire session takes a variety of forms and becomes much more fluid and diffused. Students receive feedback and feed-forward from the tutor as well as from each other as members of a connected sharing and learning community.

No marks are given for the quality of teaching and the material created. This could be seen as a weakness but equally it could be argued that it can also encourage students to be freer in experimenting without the fear of being formally assessed. Moreover, outcomes to date prove that the sense of collective

Chapter 8

responsibility which students feel within their work-groups and towards the class act as effective motivational devices to keep students on track.

3.   Results and discussion

From a pedagogical perspective, the average quality of tutorials ranged from satisfactory to high. The tutor's judgement, after observing tutorials being delivered, was that they were coherently and attentively structured, the information provided was accurate, and the exercises and activities comprehensive. The material produced showed the students' personalities and creativity. Pictures, font colours, and audio-visual materials were appropriately chosen with regard to the grammar topic and were aimed at highlighting concepts and facilitating the memorisation of rules and notions (see Figure 2).

Figure 2.   Example of video by students and grammar in context/comprehension task

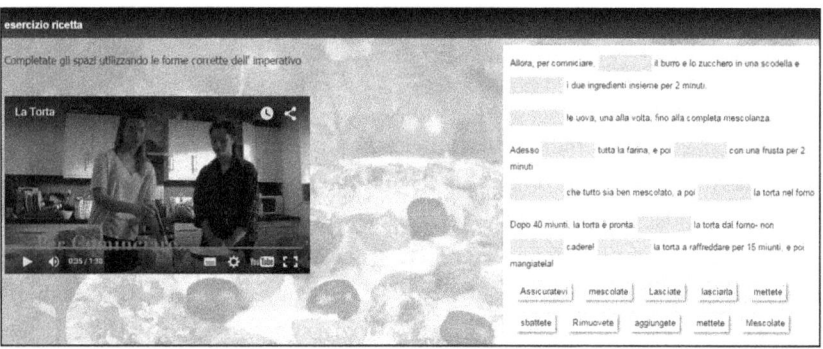

While teaching and learning grammar, students also practise all their language skills, as this work includes written and oral/aural production. Their revision of grammar is much more in-depth, since they are responsible for their classmates' learning (Boud, Cohen, & Sampson, 2001) and this impacts positively on their awareness and knowledge of the language.

Furthermore, all the tutorials are made available on the VLE after they are delivered in class, which creates a resource pool that students are encouraged to use throughout the session. These materials are also shared with the *ab initio* students, for revision purposes.

Nevertheless, some weaknesses were also noted, mainly related to the students' presentation and teaching skills: most of them had never had any previous teaching experience, hence, especially in the initial stages, they lacked confidence and needed appropriate training and guidance from the tutor and additional practice. In the first term, most students underestimated the importance of their own performance and found lesson delivery challenging. From our observations, students experienced the most difficulty when having to face the classroom and handle their classmates' queries. The 'affective filter' (Krashen, 1982) also influences both 'student-teachers' and 'student-learners', sometimes preventing interactions from being fluid. Thus, the presentation may be weak and the transmission of information not always clear. In the second term, students are much more prepared and aware of what to expect; the group work is organised and structured more accurately; they tend to be less intimidated by their classmates. Furthermore, they perceive a sense of community, relationships are tighter and interactions much more fun and constructive.

3.1. Student feedback

Collection of data consisted of questionnaires[3] submitted by all students at mid and end point to assess students' satisfaction. Interviews were also carried out, including with students at the end of the second year.

According to the qualitative feedback, most students involved in this project enjoyed the group work, in terms of planning and teaching, creating exercises and activities, and performing. Most of them stated that the peer-teaching combined with Xerte added value to their learning experience, helped them to reinforce

---

3. See sample questionnaire at https://research-publishing.box.com/s/qowhibvpppge1oqruai19kq881y1gf68

their prior knowledge of the subject, increased their confidence, and created a varied, enjoyable and relaxing learning environment. Students acknowledged the interactive features of the software as a relevant contribution to the active participation of all the learners.

Although overall student satisfaction was 100%, a small percentage expressed unease over the use of technology involved in the course. They claimed not to be sufficiently competent with technology and in some cases they questioned its educational value. Although the number of students detached from technology was very small, their opinions were generally very strong. This highlights that assumptions about the new generation of students being 'digital natives' (Prensky, 2001) should not go unchallenged. Teacher-level barriers and school-level barriers related to the use of technology have been studied (Bingimlas, 2009), yet more attention needs to be paid to student-level barriers in the context of higher education.

4. Conclusion

Learning grammar through the medium of teaching has encouraged a more participatory and active attitude towards the subject. While it is problematic to quantify the learning gains due to the lack of suitable conditions for comparison, qualitative data confirm that the aim of increasing student satisfaction and engagement was achieved and suggests the same pedagogic principles could be adapted to other teaching and learning contexts.

Future implementations and developments of the project could incorporate a stronger element of teacher training, to overcome some of the difficulties encountered in the delivery of certain aspects of the curriculum. This could especially suit more advanced students. Finally, we believe that the scope and nature of the project make it adaptable to other languages and environments and we hope it can inspire experimentation in an area – grammar – where traditional assumptions on what and how to teach are particularly entrenched in the profession.

References

Anderson, L., & Krathwohl, D. (Eds.) (2001). *A taxonomy for learning, teaching, and assessing: a revision of Bloom's taxonomy of educational objectives*. Longman.

Bingimlas, K. A. (2009). Barriers to the successful integration of ICT in teaching and learning environments: a review of literature. *Eurasia Journal of Mathematics, Science and Technology Education*, 5(3), 235-245. https://doi.org/10.12973/ejmste/75275

Boud, D., Cohen, R., & Sampson, J. (2001). *Peer learning in higher education: learning from and with each other*. Kogan Page Limited.

Falchikov, N. (2001). *Learning together: peer tutoring in higher education*. Routledge. https://doi.org/10.4324/9780203451496

Jones, L. (2007). *The student-centered classroom*. Cambridge University Press.

Krashen, S. (1982). *Principles and practice in second language acquisition*. Prentice-Hall International.

Kress, G., & Selander, S. (2012). Multimodal design, learning and cultures of recognition. *The Internet and Higher Education*, 15(4), 265-268. https://doi.org/10.1016/j.iheduc.2011.12.003

Marsh, D. (2012). *Blended learning creating learning opportunities for language learners*. Cambridge University Press.

Prensky, M. (2001). Digital natives, digital immigrants. *On the Horizon* 9(5), 1-6. https://doi.org/10.1108/10748120110424816

UCML. (2014). *Language Teaching Survey Report 2014*. http://www.ucml.ac.uk/sites/default/files/pages/160/UCML%20language%20survey%20report%202014.pdf

Whitman, N. (1988). *Peer teaching - to teaching is to learn twice*. ASHE-ERIC Higher Education Report no. 4. http://files.eric.ed.gov/fulltext/ED305016.pdf

Worton, M. (2009). *Review of modern foreign languages provision in higher education in England*. HEFCE Issues Papers 2009/41. www.hefce.ac.uk/media/hefce1/pubs/hefce/2009/0941/09_41.pdf

9. The digital world as a topic: developing digital competences in the Italian language class

Rosalba Biasini[1]

Abstract

According to the Joint Information Systems Committee (JISC) framework for digital capabilities (JISC, 2013), Information Communication Technology (ICT) proficiency is only one of the elements necessary to equip Higher Education (HE) students to fully engage with today's digital world. On its own, however, it is not enough. As ICT users, students should be encouraged not solely to use digital technologies proficiently, but also to reflect on the digital world and on their experience of it, by considering the impact of ICT in their life as well as in their learning. In this article, I will explain how digital technologies and competences can be used in the Italian language class as a topic. In order to do so, I will focus on a second year module for ex-beginner Italian students – Common European Framework of Reference for languages (CEFR) B1/B2 –, describing how, while developing all 'canonical' linguistic skills, students can improve transferable skills, such as working on self-development, shaping their digital identity and reputation, and approaching media literacies and learning. After a brief description of the context, including students' levels and needs, and of the objectives of the proposed teaching unit, I will outline how I designed the activities and approached the topic with the class, analysing the students' responses and outcomes.

Keywords: digital world, ICT proficiency, topics in language learning, transferable skills.

---

1. University of Liverpool, Liverpool, United Kingdom; rosalba.biasini@liverpool.ac.uk

How to cite this chapter: Biasini, R. (2018). The digital world as a topic: developing digital competences in the Italian language class. In R. Biasini & A. Proudfoot (Eds), *Using digital resources to enhance language learning – case studies in Italian* (pp. 95-105). Research-publishing.net. https://doi.org/10.14705/rpnet.2018.24.801

Chapter 9

1. Introduction

Students currently in HE programmes are part of the so-called 'Y generation', young people who were born and educated in the digital era and have spent their lives surrounded by and using technological tools. Yet despite being considered "digital natives", i.e. "native speakers of the digital language of computers, video games and the Internet" (Prensky, 2001, p. 1), many have only a partial perception of the potential of the digital world, often limited to the use of technological media such as PCs, smartphones, tablets, and apps (see for example Kennedy, Judd, Churchward, & Gray, 2008, a response to Prensky, 2001). This implies that, although able to use digital 'products', younger generations might not fully engage with their potential, failing for instance to understand the importance of developing media literacies that would help them in and beyond university.

The non-profit organisation JISC – which supports HE by providing advice on digital resources and technology services – has proposed a model for digital capabilities that suggests several areas linked to ICT proficiency in which students should gain appropriate skills to become both intellectually aware of all the implications of the world they live in and fully operational within it (see Figure 1).

As recommended by the JISC framework, ICT proficiency is only one of the elements necessary "to enable people in [HE] to fully [exploit] the possibilities of modern digital empowerment, content and connectivity" (JISC, 2013, n.p.). As ICT users, HE students should then be encouraged not solely to use digital technologies proficiently, but also to reflect on the digital world and on their experience of it, by considering the impact of ICT in their lives and in their learning.

Many papers in this publication deal with how digital competencies can be developed and improved, and with how both class and independent learning can be enhanced via an informed use of technologies. In this paper, I will explore how the digital world can be used in the Italian language class as a topic, informing content while promoting personal development.

Figure 1. JISC (2013) framework[2]

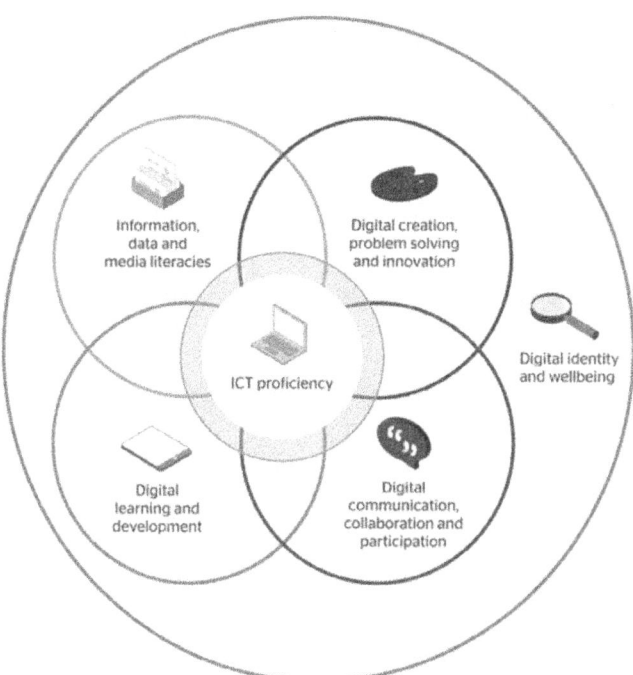

To provide an example of this practice, I will focus on a second year ex-beginner Italian module (CEFR B1/B2), describing how, while developing linguistic and digital competencies, students can also improve transferable skills, e.g. by working on self-development, shaping digital identity, and approaching media literacies and technology enhanced learning. In designing the Teaching Unit (TU) that I will discuss, I have considered how media education (or literacy) (Weyland, 2003) is more complex than generally perceived[3]. Teaching *with* the

---

2. https://www.jisc.ac.uk/guides/developing-students-digital-literacy

3. My approach in designing TUs follows Balboni's (1994, 2002, 2013) model; in English, see Balboni (2007), a "complex linguistic, communicative tranche, realised by bringing together cultural models, communicative acts, language expressions and language structures, all linked by a situational [...] or [...] grammatical context"; it is "characterised by three phases that recall the three moments of perception" - globalising > analysing > synthesising – described by the Gestalt psychology as a sequential process, "plus an initial motivational phase and a concluding one of testing and evaluation"; TUs are divided into "learning units, each one lasting for a single session" focussed on the student perception of their own learning (Balboni 2007, pp. 39-42).

media (i.e. using them as tools) and *on* the media (i.e. using them as content) are two approaches of technology enhanced teaching, along with teaching (and learning) *inside* the media (Martini, 2004). This last aspect considers all media, new technologies as well as books, as a normal, integral part of life, each with an area of action and meaning in constant interaction with each other. If, as Margiotta (1997) argues, today's student is a 'multi-literate' person ('multi-alfabeta') who possesses the ability to experience the world through different media, using the different languages employed by such tools, a fuller education must stimulate students not only to use but also to learn about the media and their 'alphabets', to provide concrete experiences of the digital world that can shape their identity.

2. Methodology

2.1. Studying Italian at Liverpool

Before outlining the project that informs this paper, the context in which Italian is taught at the University of Liverpool (UoL) should be described. As in many institutions in the UK, the Italian cohort is divided into two strands for the first two years:

- beginners (ex-Beginners in second year): an intensive pathway which prepares students for reaching level B1/B2 in their first year. This is a successful programme at UoL and constitutes the larger of the two intakes for Italian; and

- advanced: a pathway designed for students with A-level (or equivalent) competence in Italian.

After a year spent abroad, the two groups merge in their final year. Since the 2014-15 academic year, the Faculty of Humanities and Social Sciences have launched a flexible programme of study, Honours Select (HS), which allows students to combine subjects offered in the Faculty, choosing how much weight they have in their degree course. Currently, Italian can be studied at 100%, 75%, 50%, or 25%, thus constituting a component in a number of Joint or Major/Minor programmes[4]. With the introduction of HS, the number of students enrolling in the Beginners pathway has increased further. Since HS students can start Italian with no previous linguistic training (i.e. an A-level or equivalent in another language), there is now a wider variety in competences and expectations with consequent impacts on motivation and retention, so choosing topics that are relevant to the students' lives is paramount.

2.2. The Italian Beginners and ex-Beginners class

In the first and second year, students in the Beginners pathway take a module per semester, each comprising of four hours of class instruction and structured independent learning organised in activities available on the Virtual Learning Environment (VLE) Blackboard. Each teaching semester is 12 weeks long.

Weekly seminars are designed around thematic topics which focus on the engagement with the target culture and on the development of 'canonical' linguistic skills, both receptive (reading and listening) and productive (speaking and writing). I will refer to the weekly seminars as follows:

- *Grammar*, based on the discovery and acquisition of linguistic structures;

- *Texts*, focussed on the development of reading and writing skills;

- *Lab*, focussed on listening comprehension skills; and

- *Oral*, designed to enhance speaking and communicative skills.

All skills are practised in every seminar, although with a varied emphasis.

---

4. For more information on HS, see https://www.liverpool.ac.uk/study/undergraduate/courses/italian-ba-hons/overview/. For the structure of programmes with an Italian component and for Italian modules available at UoL, see https://www.liverpool.ac.uk/study/undergraduate/courses/honours-select/.

2.3. Bringing the students' world into the class: the digital era

Second year ex-Beginners modules are organised around several themes chosen to enhance student motivation and engagement. Each theme relates to Italian culture and society with an intercultural approach. Topics vary, and alongside migration, politics, the world of work, and life in Italy as a (foreign) student, can include 'new media'. Each topic is explored in a three-week long TU made of a Learning Unit (LU) for each seminar, for a total of 12 class hours.

The TU dedicated to new media was created as follows. In the first LU (Texts), as a motivational introduction to the topic, a short video on digital competences was viewed in class[5] (see supplementary material[6], parts a, b, and c). Students, divided in small groups, were subsequently asked to elicit their previous knowledge and opinions about the topic and then, with the help of the transcription of the video, to analyse the text, its content, and its language and medium.

The video introduced Prensky's notions of digital natives and immigrants[7], so students were also invited to reflect on their status vis-à-vis this definition.

At this stage, a reflection on the language used was encouraged, and examples of new media were elicited from the students for an active reflection on the world they experience. Then a new text was introduced, divided in smaller units and accompanied by different exercises[8] (see supplementary material[9], part d-e). Part (d) was meant for skimming for information, to confirm or correct students' views (e.g. the definition of 'new media' and the origin of the term), while part (e) – a more complex excerpt – was meant to make students reflect on

---

5. http://www.treccani.it/webtv/videos/pdnm_della_valle_nativi_digitali.html

6. https://research-publishing.box.com/s/frpyh0k2dg0i2a8rzrf7pazbu6ihtf4k

7. While digital natives are "native speakers" of the digital language, digital immigrants are "those [...] who were not born into the digital world but have, at some later point in our lives, become fascinated by and adopted many aspects of the new technology" (Prensky, 2001, pp. 1-2).

8. http://it.wikipedia.org/wiki/Nuovi_media

9. https://research-publishing.box.com/s/frpyh0k2dg0i2a8rzrf7pazbu6ihtf4k

the characteristics of the new media, introducing concepts such as 'variability' and 'transcodification'.

At the end of this first LU, students were provided with a list of new media including CDs, DVDs, chatrooms, blogs and so on, and asked to consider how these can be used for communication (see supplementary material[10], part f).

This phase made the class rethink their personal use of technologies, with room to propose creative ways of using them. Independent learning was also organised, with more related articles and vocabulary links (e.g. Quizlet[11]) available on the VLE. At home, students also worked on English expressions commonly used in Italian, looking for possible translations. These activities created the basis for the introductory phase of the next Texts seminar LU.

Meanwhile, during the LUs in the Lab seminars – held in a room equipped with Sanako software[12] that allows students to access the audio/video resource at their own pace and to interact with the tutor – other authentic materials (from YouTube and/or Italian newspapers) were used to explore the theme and to encourage a reflection on its presence in our everyday lives.

For the Oral seminar, designed to put into communicative practice the linguistic and cultural elements discovered in the week, the focus was on a specific aspect of digital competence, 'online reputation'. The expression was introduced to the students, prompting them to analyse its meaning, and once it was clarified, the class was led to consider the importance that building a strong online reputation can add to a personal and professional life. As homework, students worked on a practical task: verifying and assessing their presence on the web by using a website linked to an Italian TV programme (*Reputescion*[13]), and producing a short show and tell on their online reputation for the class.

---

10. https://research-publishing.box.com/s/frpyh0k2dg0i2a8rzrf7pazbu6ihtf4k

11. https://quizlet.com/

12. http://www.sanako.com/

13. https://www.my-reputation.it

In the second week, the Text seminar started with a recap based also on the extra materials available on the VLE to encourage students to engage with them during their independent learning. The new text analysed in class[14] (see supplementary material[15]) focussed on the importance of creating and maintaining a good web identity, with practical advice. Broken into smaller units with comprehension and reflective questions, the text favoured active reading.

For their independent learning, and as a conclusion to the TU, students were asked to write a short essay by the end of the third week (400 words) for formative assessment and feedback[16].

In the second Oral seminar, students shared findings about themselves, with the tutor breaking the ice showing how s/he appears online, starting with a Google search. Subsequently, the students had to share their views on how to build a stronger online reputation, and while talking in Italian, they also made written notes to help them during the following class debate on how to improve our online reputation[17]. Via this exercise, while practising Italian linguistic structures, students were able to further explore the potential of the digital world.

In the third and final week of the TU, a video from the Italian TV programme *Reputescion* was used in the Lab seminar (an interview with an Italian celebrity, in which their online presence is reviewed). In the Oral seminar, students discussed and drafted a list of 'dos & don'ts' for a perfect web identity, while the Text seminar was dedicated to writing: in groups, the essay title's keywords were

---

14. http://www.panorama.it/economia/opinioni/regole-gestione-reputazione-online/

15. https://research-publishing.box.com/s/m6bbdx2kbpb8tj34x4lwfct4exksibpp

16. The essay title asked students whether in the digital world TV is still a useful source of information ("I media e le notizie: la televisione fa ancora informazione? Elabora la tua risposta portando esempi della realtà italiana e di quella del tuo Paese"). For the summative assessment (600 words), one of the three essay titles engaged students with online reputation ("'L'immagine online è il nostro primo biglietto da visita'. Discuti questa affermazione, valutando l'importanza di costruirsi una solida reputazione online a livello privato e professionale. Nella tua discussione, fai riferimento soprattutto a esempi concreti, spiegando come un corretto uso delle nuove tecnologie e dei social network può contribuire a migliorare il proprio profilo lavorativo").

17. Such suggestions included deciding to open a LinkedIn account (https://www.linkedin.com), making their social media profile private, changing their public profile pictures, and so on.

analysed, useful resources were listed and shared, and an essay plan ("scaletta") was drafted to provide extra help to the students and to make sure that they would actually work on the essay, due at the end of that week.

3. Results and discussion

This TU has stimulated an informed reflection on the impact of ICT on students' personal and professional life. On the basis of the students' feedback, results have been encouraging and shown that the activities proposed provide various benefits for the students' learning and development. Acquiring digital literacy is amongst the cognitive skills listed in the most recent version of the Subject Benchmark Statement for Languages, which also recommends a focus on practical skills, e.g. being able to "access and use digital resources and social media appropriately" (Quality Assurance Agency for Higher Education, 2015, p. 17), as well as generic skills, e.g. being able to "use digital media effectively as a source of information, a means of communication and as an aid to learning" (Quality Assurance Agency for Higher Education, 2015, p. 24).

All the above skills have been reinforced via the TU here described. Students have been encouraged to take a more conscious approach to the web, including social media, and have been exposed to digital materials for learning. Some of them showed improved digital skills and awareness of the digital world, i.e. in their use of the Office package, as shown in their work submission and their emails, as well as in their comments in essays and in the end of semester questionnaires, which showed an appreciation for the topic. The tutor set the example by sharing his/her digital competences, and also with the digital texts proposed, including videos. These materials are discussed in class and analysed in terms of their relevance and reliability, educating the students to use Internet sources in an informed way. Being trained to check their sources carefully, students are better prepared to approach information with the same attention during their independent learning and research. Moreover, the digital materials retrieved are always authentic, as recommended by the Subject Benchmarks, and comprise Italian media, which have the benefit of opening up a fresh perspective on Italian culture and society. If the benefits so far described can be achieved using any topic, it must be recognised that the importance of discussing new media lies in offering the chance for students to reflect on digital competencies and literacies, including the importance of building an online reputation and protecting and enhancing their digital identity. Through this TU, students were encouraged not only to use technologies, but also to comment on their digital education and to expand and perfect their knowledge and skills, developing transferable skills that can have a significant impact on self-development and employability.

4. Conclusion

With the present paper, I described a TU that would provide students with a fuller understanding of the digital era they live in. As recognised by JISC and suggested by the Subject Benchmarks, students should be trained to employ a whole set of technologies and competences, including the ability to reflect on the digital world and on their experience of it, both in their life and in their learning. As explained, the digital world can be used in the language class as a content topic, helping students to improve their digital literacies and competences and to reflect on the impact on their learning and personal life, as well as in social and professional contexts.

The paper aimed at showing how, while developing all 'canonical' linguistic skills, students also improved their transferable skills, such as working on self-development, shaping digital identity and reputation, approaching media literacies, and learning. The level of students' engagement and their improved perception of the digital world have proved the approach successful.

References

Balboni, P. E. (1994). *Didattica dell'italiano a stranieri*. Bonacci.
Balboni, P. E. (2002). *Le sfide di Babele. Insegnare le lingue nelle società complesse*. UTET.

Balboni, P. E. (2007). Operational models for language education. *Documents in Language Teaching Methodology, 4*. http://arcaold.unive.it/bitstream/10278/2301/1/Nr.%204%20versione%20inglese.pdf

Balboni, P. E. (2013). *Fare educazione linguistica. Insegnare italiano, lingue straniere e lingue classiche*. UTET.

JISC. (2013). Developing students' digital literacy. Online. https://www.jisc.ac.uk/guides/developing-students-digital-literacy

Kennedy, G. E., Judd, T. S., Churchward, A., & Gray, K. (2008). First year students' experiences with technology: are they really digital natives? *Australasian Journal of Educational Technology 2008, 24* (1), 108-122. https://doi.org/10.14742/ajet.1233

Margiotta, U. (1997). *Pensare in rete. La formazione del multialfabeta*. CLUEB.

Martini, O. (2004). Percorsi nella didattica. In R. Maragliano (Ed.), *Nuovo manuale di didattica multimediale* (pp. 180-204). Laterza.

Prensky, M. (2001). Digital natives, digital immigrants. *On the Horizon, 9*(5). MCB University Press. https://www.marcprensky.com/writing/Prensky%20-%20Digital%20Natives,%20Digital%20Immigrants%20-%20Part1.pdf

Quality Assurance Agency for Higher Education. (2015). Subject Benchmark for Languages and Related Studies. Online. http://www.qaa.ac.uk/en/Publications/Documents/SBS-Languages-Cultures-and-Societies-15.pdf

Weyland, B. (2003). *Media scuola formazione. Esperienze, ricerche, prospettive. Quaderno di ricerca*. Praxis Verlag.

Author index

B
Biasini, Rosalba iv, 1, 3, 95

C
Campisi, Salvatore iv, 2, 43
Celant, Paola iv, 2, 29

K
Kaliska, Marta v, 2, 5

L
La Sala, Maria Chiara v, 2, 17
Lomartire, Simone v, 3, 55

M
Motzo, Anna v, 3, 67

O
Oliviero, Marcella vi, 3, 81

P
Proudfoot, Anna iv, 1

Z
Zhok, Andrea vi, 3, 81